GYULA WOJTILLA

HISTORY OF KṚṢIŚĀSTRA

GYULA WOJTILLA

HISTORY OF KṚṢIŚĀSTRA

Bibliografische Information der Deutschen Nationalbibliothek
Die Deutsche Nationalbibliothek verzeichnet diese Publikation in der Deutschen Nationalbibliografie; detaillierte bibliografische Daten sind im Internet über http://dnb.dnb.de abrufbar.

Bibliographic information published by the Deutsche Nationalbibliothek
The Deutsche Nationalbibliothek lists this publication in the Deutsche Nationalbibliografie; detailed bibliographic data are available in the internet at http://dnb.dnb.de.

For further information about our publishing program consult our website http://www.harrassowitz-verlag.de

Kreuzberger Ring 7c-d, 65205 Wiesbaden, produktsicherheit.verlag@harrassowitz.de

ISBN 978-3-447-05306-8

Contents

Preface to the second edition 7

Preface to the first edition 9

Part One. Kṛṣiśāstra literature 11
  What is kṛṣiśāstra? 11
  The origin and development of kṛṣiśāstra 15

Part Two. Individual kṛṣiśāstras (in alphabetical order) 21

Appendix One. Texts containing independent chapter(s) on kṛṣi 63

Appendix Two. Collections of agricultural sayings not attributed to authors 75

Appendix Three. Texts on tanks and wells 77

Appendix Four. Works recorded in AAI still waiting for verification 79

Bibliography and abbreviations 81

Preface
to the second edition

There have been tremendous changes in the availability of the basic texts bearing on agriculture since I published a shorter version of this book under the same title as Acta Antiqua et Archaeologica Supplementum IX (Acta Universitatis de Attila József Nominatae) in Szeged in 1999. Due to the great efforts of the Asian Agri-History Foundation established in 1994 in Secunderabad, A. P. India hitherto unpublished texts appeared with English translation and studies written by learned scholars and some basic texts gained new edition and translation. In the last five years I constantly searched for sources and tried to fill the gaps in our knowledge. The present volume comprises the main results of this painstaking work.

As to the way of the actual work I can only repeat some ideas expressed in the preface to the first edition. While working on the subject I faced several difficulties, which are obvious to all those who know how scanty information stands at our disposal. As a matter of fact one looks for information in the histories of Indian literature in vain. The only substantial work which also served as a starting point for further work in many case was the volume entitled 'Agriculture in ancient India' New Delhi 1964, Indian Council of Agricultural Research which I had the luck to buy in Benares in August 1973. The technical editor of the volume R. K. Kak, M. A. Ph.D. deserves special credits for visiting fourty-one libraries in India.

Since 1977 I have been doing research in many libraries and manuscript collections of India and several European countries in order to find unedited texts in Sanskrit and various Indian vernaculars and to consult the printed text and study the secondary literature.

There are many people to whom I would like to express my deep feeling of gratitude.

Firstly I must mention my teacher the late Prof. János Harmatta and the late Prof. Lallanji Gopal (Varanasi), who have been my benevolent inspirators since 1973. Dr R. A. Pathak my brāhmaṇa friend, and great scholar B. H. U. Department of Indology constantly helped me in 1973–1974 and 1977 and later in our correspondence both in Sanskrit and vernacular sources.

The late Prof. V. Raghavan (Madras) gave me an immense help by managing to get a copy of the Kāśyapīyakr̥ṣisūkti.

Prof. S. Sankaranarayanan, Director, S. V. U. Oriental Research Institute, Tirupati draw my attention to certain Telugu texts and gave suggestions about their age in 1977.

In tackling Malayalam texts I received great assistance from Prof. N. P. Unni of University of Kerala in Trivandrum in 1977 and from Prof. M. G. S. Narayanan of the Indian Council of Historical Research in New Delhi in 1990.

Special thanks are due to Prof. Rahul Peter Das (Halle) for procuring a copy of the Kr̥ṣiśāsana and for numerous invaluable suggestions during our talks in the last fifteen years.

I am very much indebted to Dr George F. Baumann, former Director of the Oriental Library University of Tübingen for his generous help of various kinds.

During the preparation of this second enlarged and revised edition I have received invaluable help from Prof. Y. L. Nene, Chairman, Asian Agri-History Foundation, Secunderabad, India who had presented me the the excellent publications of the Foundation and helped me especially in Telugu matters.

I should like to place on record my gratitude to Prof. Jaroslav Vacek for help in Tamil issues.

Last but not least my best thanks to Prof. Dieter P. Kapp (Köln) for taking up my work in the series *Beiträge zur Kenntnis südasiatischer Sprachen und Literaturen.* My sincere thanks are due to *Harrassowitz Verlag* for undertaking the publication of the work.

Budapest 2005

Gyula Wojtilla

Preface
to the first edition

This little book is a modest attempt to present a short history of the *kṛṣiśāstra*, a forgotten chapter in the history of technical literature in India. While working on the subject I faced several difficulties, which are obvious to all those who know how scanty the available sources for research of this nature are. Moreover, the sources are in several languages and come from quite different parts of India.

There are many people to whom I would like to express my deep feeling of gratitude.

Firstly I must mention Prof. Lallanji Gopal (Varanasi), who has been my benevolent inspirator since 1973 and who quite recently encouraged me to undertake this job.

The late Professor V. Raghavan (Madras) gave me an immense help by managing to get a copy of the Kāśyapīyakṛṣisūkti.

Special thanks are due to Prof. Rahul Peter Das (Halle) for procuring a copy of the Kṛṣiśāsana and for numerous valuable suggestions during our talks in the last ten years.

I am very much indebted to Dr George F. Baumann, Director of the Oriental Library University of Tübingen for his generous help of various kinds.

Jane and John Strong kindly checked and patiently corrected my English at several places. If there are still mistakes, the responsibility is, of course, entirely mine.

Last but not least, I am very grateful to my friends Márta and Vilmos Bojkovszky for the grant that enabled to meet the expenditures of printing.

Gyula Wojtilla

PART ONE

Kṛṣiśāstra literature

WHAT IS KṚṢIŚĀSTRA?

The first member of the compound kṛṣi has been defined as a separate branch of occupations. Kauṭilya listed it under the commulative term vārttā 'economy' (cf. Law 1918, 239) together with animal husbandry (paśupālya) and trade (vanijyā) (Arthśā I, 4,1) and MahāBhā VI, 40, 44 (= Bhagavadgītā XVIII, 44) ascribes it together with cattle-tending (gorakṣya) and trade (vanijya) to vaiśyas. The term occurs in the same sense and in the same context in the Amarakośa (AmaK II, 9, 2.) and in the great encyclopedia by Basavarāja (ŚivataRaK I, 1, 52). Amara makes a clear distinction between 'agriculture' (kṛṣi) and 'gleaning' (uñcha or śila) (AmaK II, 9, 2). According to the Mahābhāṣya it denotes not merely ploughing, but includes collectively all other operations of agriculture, such as the supply of seeds, implements, animals and human labour (MahāBh III, 1, 26. – cf. Agrawala 1963, 194). Animals are so far concerned as far they are employed in the various operations otherwise their treatment belongs to paśupālya, aśvaśāstra, gajaśāstra, gocikitsā etc. Texts bearing on the establishment of wells or ponds (kūpavidhi, taḍāgavidhi) form part of agriculture although certain kṛṣiśāstras such as the Kāśyapīyakṛṣisūkti contain chapters on such topics. For these structures may serve also another purposes the texts dealing with them are not kṛṣiśāstras proper therefore I give an account of them in an appendix.

Kṛṣiśāstra firstly denotes 'agricultural science' and, as such, it is a synonym of kṛṣitantra (Gopal 1973, 167 and Das 1988, 1.). Another synonym is sasyaveda 'the science of crops' (KṛtyaKaT DānaK p. 208.) 'die Lehre vom Ackerbau' (pw VII, 98.). According to Gode this is the title of a lost work referred to in a verse of the Nandipurāṇa, a text which itself is known only from citations in dharmanibandhas (Gode 1948, 11.). The verse in question can be interpreted in this sense although, the first meaning is more likely.

Sīrajñāna 'the knowledge of plough', or its emended form sītajñāna 'the knowledge of furrow', covers a considerably narrower semantical field (Bhaṭṭasvāmin on ArthŚā II, 24; cf. Das 1988, 1.). As Das puts it phalaveda 'the science of crops' is it the name of works the subject of which is vṛkṣāyurveda (Das 1988, 1). In this connection he refers to NyāyaMañ 64 in Āhnika 4 (p.609). On the other hand Das also quotes Cakradhara's statement: phalavedaṁ sasyapālaśāstram which we understand as 'the science of protecting crops'. This later much broader sense of the term can be corroborated from the Kashmirian NīlamaP 651: phalavedāttato jñātvā nāgavarṣasya vārakam / tasya pūjā prayoktavyā bhakṣyabhojyapuraḥsarā 'having known the day of the Nāga-year from the Phalaveda, one should worship that (day) with solid food and other articles of diet' (Ved Kumari's translation). The knowledge of phalaveda seems to be the property of astronomers (daivajña). We learn from tradition represented by such texts as the Kṛṣiparāśara that this knowledge is an essential part of the science of agriculture (kṛṣiśāstra). The term kṛṣipurāṇa 'agricultural lore' was coined by the sage Parāśara, the renowned agricultural expert, and figures as a practical name indicating a practical science which heavily depends on both great and little tradition. Daśarathaśāstrī in the introduction to his Kṛṣiśāsana calls the text kṛṣimāhātmya 'The eulogy of agriculture' a term that strictly refers to certain parts of kṛṣiśāstras proper (beginning of Kṛṣiparāśara, one chapter of Kāśyapīyakṛṣisūkti) or to whole poems (Ēreḻupatu). It is not by accident that this science ambiguously got into the taxonomy of sciences, The Prasthānabheda of Madhusūdana which otherwise enumerates among others horse-breeding, science of arts and mechanics, science of cooking belonging to arthaśāstra keeps silent on it (cf. Deussen 1920, 61). There is a tradition recorded in the introduction (upodghāta, p.1) to the edition of the Kāśyapaśilpa which treats kṛṣiśāstra as the first among the ten śāstras. Kṛṣiśāstra must be distinguished from vṛkṣāyurveda, 'the science about the life-span of trees', or vṛkṣāyuryoga, used perhaps in the same sense by Vātsyāyana (KāmaSū I, 3, 15; cf. Das, 1988, 1). Bhatṭṭasvāmin in his commentary on Arthaśāstra II, 24, 1 ascribes the science called vṛkṣāyurveda to Agniveśa (Wojtilla 1997–1998, 676). While vṛkṣāyurveda belongs to the group of the sixty-four kalās agriculture does not (KāmaSū I, 3; Śr̥ṅgāPra p. 969; Das 1988, 2; KalāVi IV, 10: vr̥kṣakalā). As a synonym of these two there is the word upavanavinoda, 'the pleasure of groves'. An independent work being an extract from the Śārṅgadharapaddhati bears this title indeed (Majumdar 1935). These three altogether represent 'arboriculture' and 'horticulture' in Indian tradition, as they do in modern times.

Kr̥ṣiśāstra secondly means 'a textbook of agriculture' including theoretical and practical knowledge concerning agriculture. In reality texts labelled kr̥ṣiśāstras in Sanskrit or in vernaculars embrace a wider scope of topics related to village life and have an encyclopedical character, often comprising agriculture, animal husbandry and veterinary science, arbori- and horticulture and even passages that may fit into dharmaśāstras or arthaśāstras. In short, it is easier to say what kr̥ṣiśāstra is not than to say what is. Such texts as Gurusaṁhitā, Meghamālā, Lokavijayayantra, Vatsaraphala, Vanamālā, Varṣalakṣaśa and Saṁvatsaraphala have traditionally been labelled as texts on natural astronomy (jyotiṣa). Viśvavallabha is called in the colophon āyurveda. It does not mean that 'real' kr̥ṣiśāstra passages occur in the Gurusaṁhitā (Gopal 1981, 47) or in the Lokavijayayantra (verses 9, 10, 14, 17, 18, 22 and 27). In Gopal's words 'The early medieval period, which witnessed large farms as a result of the feudalised economy and state structure, created a deeper interest in agriculture and its problems. For catering to the needs of the class of landed aristocracy a number of Sanskrit texts on agriculture, particularly weather-forecasting, were prepared in the period' (Gopal 1980, 1). The short text called Aṅkurārpaṇavidhi, 'The method of acquiring sprouts' extant in several manuscripts in South India (cf. CC I, 4), is a book of Vaiṣṇava ritual therefore I do not include it in the present book. The Viśvallabha has mixed contents: there are chapters on wells, irrigation, arbori- and horticulture but there are also passages that bear on agriculture.

It seems reasonable to accept as a working hypothesis that kr̥ṣiśāstras are those texts, irrespective of their mixed contents, which include the word kr̥ṣi in their title, or a synonym of it, or those that are agreed upon in Indian tradition as such. Ēr̥lupatu, Kāśyapīyakr̥ṣisūkti, Kr̥ṣigītā, Kr̥ṣicakraṅṅal, Kr̥ṣijñānapradīpikā, Kr̥ṣipāṭṭu,

Kr̥ṣiparāśara, Kr̥ṣiviṣayaka, Kr̥ṣiśāsana, Kr̥ṣisamayanirṇaya, Kedārakalpa, Kṣetratattva, Kṣetraprakāśa, Cāṣāpālā, Nuskha dar fann -i-falāhat, Sasyanandamu, Sasyānanda and on the other hand Khanār-bocan, Ghāgh aur Bhaḍḍarī kī kahāvateṅ, Tirukkaivalakkam, Ḍāker-bocan are examples of those.

THE ORIGIN AND DEVELOPMENT OF KṚṢIŚĀSTRA

As a matter of fact not any extant kṛṣiśāstra antedates the early medieval times. It does not mean that texts containing information about agricultural science it did not exist before that period. The Sītādhyakṣaprakaraṇa of the Arthaśāstra (ArthŚā II, 41) obviously presupposes certain literature or at least certain knowledge on the level of theory or science. Bhaṭṭotpala in his commentary on that chapter appears to know the school of this science represented by Vṛddhaparāśara and others. Similarly the Bṛhatsaṁhitā (BṛSaṁ chapter 40) is also familiar with this type of literature and science. The respective chapters bearing on agricultural-like activities in the Agnipurāṇa (AgniP ch. 121) may preserve earlier material on the subject, too. It is a question whether these texts are earlier than the oldest extant kṛṣiśāstras. There is a remarkable coincidence between the appearance of kṛṣiśāstras as a literary genre and the literary form both in Indo-Aryan and Dravidian languages and the extension of cultivated territories (cf. Wojtilla 1991a, 163–165) in which agricultural experience met the theoretical knowledge of brāhmaṇas. In early medieval times – as Kosambi puts it – 'they acted as pioneers in undeveloped localities; they first brought plough agriculture to replace slash-and-burn cultivation, or food-gathering. New crops, knowledge of markets, organisation of village settlements and trade also came with them' (Kosambi 1970, 172). Their role becomes visible in the coining of Sanskritised terms of agriculture, supplying theoretical knowledge of astronomy, botany, economy and law and codifying popular wisdom deposited, for example, in the collections of sayings in vernaculars. The relatively sophisticated methods of cultivation required a great number of beasts of burden, especially cattle, a circumstance that raised the prestige of the cow, and made their higher protection inevitable, especially in those areas of India where vegetarianism was not an established custom. The propagation of ritually pure food fit for offering to the gods and for everyday meals of the higher castes cannot be separated from the more differentiated agricultural and horticultural activities. The importance of agriculture suddenly emerged: Kṛṣiparāśara verse 6 states: 'Rice is vitality, rice is vigour too, and rice (indeed) is the fulfilment of all ends (of life). Gods, demons and human beings all subsist on rice.' The legitimitation of king in the regional kingdoms, which was strongly promoted by brāhmaṇas, designated a special role for the kings. In certain regions the kings appear to be the highest patrons of agriculture. The verses 1–3 of the Kāśyapīyakṛṣisūkti read thus: 'For the sake of pleasing the Gods, the pious king – who bears the burden of protecting his subjects – having punished the wrongdoers and establishing the law entirely should give nourishment to those subjects of good behaviour who are devoted to the system of the varṇāśrama. The Gods, spirits, heavenly choristers, fathers, sages and others are said to be meritorious of the different sacrifices. The wise men knew that they could please them by devayajña.' After A. D. 600 certain authors of lawbooks such as Parāśara (see Parāśarasmṛti) and Devala permit even the brāhmaṇas themselves to take to the cultivation of land. Although they commit a kind of sin they can put right it by giving one-sixth of the crop to the king one-twentieth to the gods and one-thirtieth to brāhmaṇas learned in the Vedas (Ritschl 1980, 186).

As to the composition of the extant kṛṣiśāstra literature, the opinions of scholars vary. De concludes that the Kṛṣiparāśara is 'a Sanskrit version of the collective weather-wisdom of the popular vernacular proverbs' (De 1960, II). Although the title Kāśyapīya-kṛṣisūkti seems to offer another example, the matter is not so simple. The term sūkti indicates sayings moreover – as we shall see – the style and the loose redaction allows us to think of a collection of sayings rather than of a śāstra proper but there is not any indication that these sayings have been translated from any vernacular. The origin of the Bengali literature of this kind goes back to a remote past. Dasgupta surmises it is of foreign origin and believes that the traditional wisdom of the agricultural people of Malabar is the possible source (Dasgupta 1935, 224 and 225 n. 1.). Special attention was paid in former days to the study of astrology and astronomy, and what is also interesting, 'Tantric form of worship is common to both the Nambutiris and Bengali brahmans' (Drav. Enc. II, 529). The prominent Malabar school of astronomy and the provenance of such texts as the Kṛṣicakraṅṅal, Kṛṣisamayanirṇaya and Varṣalakṣaṇa and considerable portions of the Kṛṣigītā seem to underline this hypothesis. As Burton Stein says 'proven techniques, tools, seed varieties, and timings of certain operations are transmitted over time in songs and proverbs so that a catalogue of agricultural proverbs can probably be compared to the Sanskrit literary genre, sūtra in being an outline of reflective and orally transmitted knowledge' (Stein 1994, 25). It is another question as to how far the science of climatology was influenced by strictly theoretical knowledge and popular wisdom. Gopal, having analysed the contents of the Gurusaṁhitā speaks of the great importance of the Sanskrit sources of this kind of knowledge (Gopal 1981, IV). Dh. Tripathi goes further when he states that vernacular texts on weather-forecasting are translations from Sanskrit and that this work was executed by paṇḍits in the eighteenth century (Tripathi 1971, 6–7).

It is true that climatology, based on astronomy, or even rain-making, based on magic, form an essential art of agriculture and consequently of the kṛṣiśāstras. This branch of science can be traced back to the Vedas. It appears, for instance, in a hymn addressed to Mitra-Varuṇa (ṚV, 5, 63), in the relevant portion of the Buddhist literature Mahāmāyūrī ('The peacock spell'), Meghasūtra ('Cloud sermon' cf. Schmithausen 1997, 56–58) and later Bṛhatsaṁhitā (BṛSaṁ ch. 46 and 47). Greek accounts on ancient India observe that this science and the related subjects were the privileges of the brāhmaṇas. As Arrian puts it: 'Alone of the Indians they are expert in prophecy, and none save a sophist is allowed to prophesy. They prophesy only about the seasons of the year and any public calamity' (Indike ll, 4–5., P. A. Brunt's translation). Similarly the establishment of irrigational systems demanded learned persons. Kāśyapīyakṛṣisūkti speaks of water-finders who are conversant with the kṛṣiśāstra (KKSū 683). This statement is well in line with the respective descriptions of the Bṛhatsaṁhitā (BṛSaṁ ch. 54.). The planning of dams, sluices, channels and water reservoirs required engineering experts. At the same time Parāśara reminds us of a kind of lore we should not forget that certain departments of agricultural science belong to the applied sciences rather than to the experimental sciences. Such terms as kṛṣikarmavid 'knower of agricultural work' (KKSū 633), kṛṣikovida 'skilled in agriculture' (KKSū 457 and 558) kṛṣipaddhatikovida 'skilled in the manuals for agriculture' (KKSū 110), or kṛṣivicakṣaṇa 'experienced in agriculture' (KKSū 586) suggest this practical aspect of agriculture. Certain operations were obviously based on observations therefore it is not by accident that the prescriptions concerned are the same in popular sayings and śāstric texts. Kṛṣiparāśara reads: 'The sowing of seeds for transplantation is said to be best in Āṣāḍha' (Majumdar–Banerji 1960) and 'thus following Khanā it is believed that sowing paddy seeds within the first five days of the month of Āṣāḍh (May–June) will yield much crop' (Dasgupta 1935, 226). Of course both texts can be connected with the same region namely north-eastern India, especially Bengal. Daśarathasvāmin, the author of Kṛṣiśāsana, who drew mainly from Sanskrit sources included the advices of his friends who were farmers. The presence of deśī-words, or obviously Sanskritised ones, in the inventory of tools cannot be overlooked (Kuiper 1969, 213–216; Wojtilla 1985, 200; Wojtilla 1988).

To sum up, kṛṣiśāstra is essentially an applied science and has many facets. Climatology and related subjects as well as irrigation together with botany, veterinary sciences or economic law appear in them together with experimental knowledge. There is a counteraction between the elements of agricultural knowledge derived from the 'great tradition' and 'little tradition'. It is a uniquely masterful work that brāhmaṇas codified a great deal of this knowledge in Sanskrit or in vernaculars. The making of a śāstric character of the Sanskrit texts also praises the high quality of their editorial work. These endeavours resulted in composing a fair number of textbooks and didactical poems. The śāstras have their distinctive features of śāstric literature in general; this circumstance explains for instance the attribution of certain texts to gods, semi-gods or mythical sages. (cf. Pollock 1985). Of course the importance of such attributions must not be overrated because at times they were in linbe with the common practice without any responsibility therefore such ascriptions were sometimes of little value (Das 1997, 205). The survival of collections of popular sayings in Bengali, Hindi, Marathi, Rajasthani or dialects of them point to the common roots and properly demonstrates the vital importance of the 'little tradition'. The great number of individual sayings spread over the huge folkloristic literature bear the testimony that Indian folklore continues to be a constant source of kṛṣiśāstra. Likewise editorial work of learned authors did not come to a halt for instance Daśarathaśāstri composed his Kṛṣiśāsana in 1909.

PART TWO

Individual kṛṣiśāstras

(in alphabetical order)

Ēreḻupatu

Lang.: Tamil

Ed.: – with the commentary of Tirunagantaiyar by Velayudha Madaliar, Madras, 1886 – Kampar nūlkal iyaṟṟiya. 3. Ēr-eḻupatu. Ceṇṇai [Madras], 1969.

Lit.: Nilakanta Sastri 1955^2 – Jesudasan 196l, 183. – AAI 165. – Zvelebil 1975, 185. – Wojtilla 1982a, 170. – Zvelebil 1995, 319.

The poem called 'The seventy stanzas on the plough', which dates from the 11th century, praises the plough and the ploughmen. It has been ascribed to Kamban, but it does not show anything like the Kamban touch. (Jesudasan 1961, 183). The attribution of the authorship to Kamban is in accordance with the tendency to ascribe minor works of unknown origin to celebrated authors (Zvelebil 1975, 185. cf. Vacek). Even the Colamaṇḍalaśataka by Atmanathar Desikar of Velur (1650–1728) verse 38 recalls with pride the support which the ancient Choliyar (= sāt śūdras, a cultivator caste) gave to Kamban who produced this hymn to the plough and to the Vellalas (Nilakanta Sastri 1955^2, 672).

Kāśyapīyakṛṣisūkti

Lang.: Sanskrit

Mss.: A Devanāgarī manuscript kept at the Adyar Library in Chennai (Madras) under the signature TR-871-63419-XXXVIII.1-8). Its colophon reads thus: transcribed by pandit V. Vijayaraghavacharya, epigraphist, Tirupati S. India on 19th December 1930. The lines or verses in it are unnumbered. All my efforts and that of other scholars failed to trace the manuscript the transcript had been made from. Ayachit wrongly calls it a Tamil manuscript (Ayachit–Sadhale–Nene 2002, vii.). In fact there is only a short glossary of vegetable names with Tamil equivalents on pp. 20–21. Page numbers are given but lines of verses are not numbered. A transcript of the Adyar manuscript belongs to Sri G. G. Joshi Pratisthan of Nagpur. It is numbered by the copyist. The copy is much inferior to the Adyar manuscript because the scribe obviously misread the Adyar manuscript and at many places put numerous errors in the text.

Ed.: Kāśyapīyakṛṣisūkti: A Sanskrit work on agriculture I. Ed. by Gy. Wojtilla. In: AOH 33:2 (1979), 209–252. – Kashyapiyakrishisukti (A treatise on agriculture by Kashyapa) translated by S. M. Ayachit, commentaries by Nalini Sadhale and Y. L. Nene. Secunderabad 2002 (Agri-History Bulletin 4). It is an edition in Devanāgarī script based on a transcript by Pandit V. N. Sastri and was checked together with Sri N. R. Bhat from the single extant manuscript kept at the Adyar Library, Chennai (Madras). This copy belongs to Sri G. G. Joshi Pratisthan of Nagpur and bears the No. 38J8 (hereinafter: Ayachit–Sadhale–Nene 2002). It is a pity that the manuscript contains numerous scribal errors. The editor published the manuscript in a facsimile and put the correct readings taken from the Adyar manuscript in footnotes.

Trans.: AAI (excerpts) – Randhawa 1980 (excerpts) – Kāśyapīyakṛṣisūkti: A Sanskrit work on agriculture II. English translation by Gy. Wojtilla. In: AOH 39:1 (1985), 84–136. (complete). – Ayachit–Sadhale–Nene 2002).

Lit.: Gode 1943, 170 and 173. – Ayachit–Sadhale–Nene 2002 passim – AAI 158 – Randhawa 1980, 484 ff. – Wojtilla 1982a, 165–166. – Wojtilla 1995. – Wojtilla 2002. – Wojtilla forthcoming.

This is the largest extant text on agriculture in Sanskrit. The treatise is traditionally ascribed to Kāśyapamuṇi, the sage Kāśyapa who had received the text from the goddess Bhūdevī and the later from Brahmā. The work is known only from the manuscript kept at the Adyar Library, Chennai (Madras). Unfortunately, neither the mythical origin nor the manuscript helps us to trace the exact provenance or date of the text. What can be said is that the single extant copy was made by a Tamil or Telugu (?) speaking scribe but this fact does not throws much light on the origin of the work itself. A further difficulty is that no quotations from it have so far turned up in other works, not even oblique references. On the other hand there are citations from various authorities (Bhārgava verses

211, 536–537); however, they cannot be identified with the verses attributed to him in the Nītikalpataru by Kṣemendra (NītiKaT verses 58–61 and 98.). Therefore we have to think of a forgotten line of tradition. It is an intricating question as to whether this Bhārgava has anything to do with Bhārgava Rāma alias Paraśurāma who instructed Kerala brāhmaṇas on agriculture in the Malayalam text Kṛṣigītā (Gārgya verses 65–66.) and Nārada the yogi (verses 350–351.). The compound kṛṣipaddhatikovida (verse 110) may give a hint to the textbook Kṛṣiparāśara a manuscript of which bears this name; however, we could not find any passages taken from that book in the Kāśyapīyakṛṣisūkti. These passages are of no value for dating our text. The mention of the pākaśāstra, authored by Nala, and another one by Bhīmasena are of little help. Bhīmasena as a specialist of sūdaśāstra, i. e. the science of the kitchen, is referred to in the Bṛhatkāthaślokasaṁgraha of Budhasvāmin (BṛKaŚlSaṁ XVI, 61 and XVIII, 20), a text dated from the eighth–ninth centuries (Banerji 1971, 169). King Nala was a famous cook, according to the epic tradition. A booklet on cooking under his name called Pākadarpaṇa 'Mirror of cooking' has survived (Wojtilla 2004). This text is extant in variant readings and one of them was printed in Benares in 1915. The dating of it is not without problems, but since red pepper is not mentioned in the book, it must have been written before the introduction of chili to India in the seventeenth century (Masica 1979, 123). The third main chapter concerning the preparation of ritually pure food recommended for the brāhmaṇas borrows a great deal from the Mānavadharmaśāstra (ManuSm V, 5–26.) and the Vaikhānasasmārtasūtra (VaikhaSmS IX, 15). According to W. Caland the editors of the former might have known the latter (Caland 1929, XIX). In that case we may suspect a long chain of Vaikhānasa tradition from the ancient times up to the time when the Kāśyapīyakṛṣisūkti was edited. Notwithstanding we must proceed with utmost care because too many details in the history of the Vaikhānasas are still in almost total darkness. Some specialists of the Vaikhānasa tradition argue that the relation of the Kāśyapīyakṛṣisūkti to the Vaikhānasa literature cannot be ascertained without further research (Personal communications from T. Goudriaan and G. Colas). The existence of a text called Kāśyapajñānakāṇḍa, 'The wisdom-book of Kāśyapa', from the Tirupati area dated in the second half of the first millennium A. D. (Goudriaan 1965, 10) is also of no use; because there is no sound evidence of a closer relation between this and our text. On the basis of a reference to Kośala as the best paddy producing area (verse 424) Randhawa proposes a date between the 5th and 10th centuries A. D. (Randhawa 1980, 484). We learn from the Rāmāyaṇa II, 100, 45 that Kosala is an adevamātṛka country where agriculture is based on artificial irrigation assured by sufficient rain. Another attempt at dating can be made if we pursue the name Kāśyapa in agricultural tradition. As a cultural hero, promoter of cultivation, his name can safely be attested to in the Arthaśāstra (ArthŚā II, 24, 27), Rājataraṅgiṇī (RājaT V, 113), Nīlamatapurāṇa (NīlamaP 300), and Bhaṭṭotpala, in his commentary on Bṛhatsaṁhitā LIV, 7 calls him an expert in agricultural meteorology. J. J. Meyer holds that the first attestation of the name can be found in the Pāraskaragṛhyasūtra (PāraGS II, 13; cf. Meyer 1937, 157, note. 1); however the identification of Udālakakāśyapa with the semi-god invoked in the mantra in the locus citated from the Arthaśāstra remains a question. Since Kāśyapa in the Kāśyapīyakṛṣisūkti does not figure as an astronomer or climatologist the information given by Bhaṭṭotpala does not concern our Kāśyapa. Because the Rājataraṅgiṇī and the Nīlamatapurāṇa are Kashmirian texts, they preserve a very valuable tradition about Kāśyapa, who regulated the rivers and made cultivation in the Kashmir valley possible. It is interesting to note that his expertise in canalisation has been equally highlighted in the Kashmirian texts and the Kāśyapīyakṛṣisūkti. On the other hand we must contend with the possibility that there was an accidental similarity between the irrigation systems in Kashmir and in the territory of the late Pallava kingdom where the patronage of paddy cultivation was a prominent task of the kings following the Vaiṣṇava faith (Gonda 1954, 236). In addition Tirupati – the place to where the provenance of the single manuscript can be traced – was the centre of the Vaikhānasas excelled also in grain (paddy) cultivation from the early medieval times onward. The last word can be said only after one has a better knowledge of the history of the Vaikhānasas. One striking phenomenon of the religious views depicted in our text is the Varāha incarnation of Viṣṇu and the lengthy treatment of the myth of Viṣṇu–Varāha and Bhūdevī the earth-goddess. The appearance of this myth in South Indian religious tradition and as a popular topic in the fine art in the early medieval period suggests that our text is related to the same age. It is in harmony with the date c. 700–800 A. D. proposed by Nene (Ayachit–Sadhale–Nene 2002, 132). Simultaneously there are passages in the text that indicate late interpolations: for instance, the mentioning of seemingly modern botanical taxonomy. The list of foods offered to gods is also of some help in locating or dating the text. Among others Nene draws attention to temana (837) a soup made from curd in Karnataka since 1200 A. D. and jalepikā (833) which he regards different from Arabic zalabiya (Ayachit–Sadhale–Nene 2002, 144). First of all I must mention that jalepikā is a Sanskritised form of the vernacular jalebī. As to the latter I may refer to Gode's research in the history of this sweetmeat. According to Gode it is a corruption of the Arabic zalābīya, Persian zalībiya and it is a rich sweetmeat made of sugar and ghee, with a little flour, melted and trickled into a pan so as to form a kind of interlaced work when baked. The dish was unknown in India prior to the seventeenth century (Gode 1943, 170 and 173). The analysis of the language and style has brought minimum result. There are few Middle-Indo-Aryan forms which are Kosala (verse 321: instead of Sanskrit Kośala), pādaghaṭṭanaka 'threshing by feet' (verse 487) and pānaghaṭṭa 'the bank of a canal' (verse 94). In addition kheṭa 'paring plough' (verse 414 cf. Wojtilla 1985, 200) is a deśī-word. Certain words may also be of some help. Pecana is perhaps a wrong form which cannot be attested in any Sanskrit lexicon. Ayachit emended it for peṣaṇa 'pounding' (Ayachit–Sadhale–Nene 2002, 104), once I proposed preṅkhana 'swinging', 'shaking', a motion in the process of winnowing and ascribed the mistake to Telugu influence: Telugu pecu means 'to clean', 'peel', 'rind' (Wojtilla 1995, 272 and Brown 1980, 791). Śaṅkula (480) 'sickle' does not occur in any Sanskrit text known to me. Śaṅkulā f. 'a kind of lancet or knife', 'a pair of nippers or scissors (used to cut the areca-nut into small pieces)' (MW 1047). Curiously, the form śaṅkula occurs in Telugu in the sense 'chisel', 'nut-cracker' and it is regarded as a Sanskrit loanword (Brown 1980, 1247). Sadhale points to the appearance of southern orthography in the form gumbhita instead of the expected gumphita (Ayachit–Sadhale–Nene 2002, 130). On the contrary, vernacular jalebī has been Sanskritised as jalepikā. To sum up, there are different textual layers in the work. The earliest one can be dated from the post-Gupta times i. e. after the sixth century A. D. when the bulk of peasantry came from the śūdras (cf. Kosambi 1970, 172) as it is depicted in our work. Later interpolations might have entered into the text. As to the provenance of the present text, we cannot ignore the testimony of two lists of geographical names: Kāśmīra, Vaṅga, Nepāla, Pañcāla, Kośala, Kuru, Virāṭa, Avanti, Mālava, Śakadeśya, Sindhu-Sauvīra, Cedi, Koṅkāna, Andhra (verses 321–322) and Gandhāra, Kunti, Pañcāla, Kāśmīra, Avanti, Sindhu, Nepāla, Naiṣadha, Kośala, Aṅga, Ghūrjara, Saurāṣṭra (verses 751–752). The form Ghūrjara shows southern influence: in Telugu Ghūrjaramu is the name of Gujerat (Brown 1980, 401). These names delineate a territory extending to the end of Andhra while vast lands of the South are missing. It is curious because we learn from the Mahābhārata (MahāBhā XII, 49, 56) that Paraśurāma having defeated the kṣatriyas presented South India Kāśyapa as a gratuity for the sacrifice of a horse. Nene suggests with a considerable argumentation that the main focus of Kashyapa was the Krishna-Godavari deltas and the adjacent areas: the region described by Kashyapa has assured rainfall to fill up reservoirs; clayey red to black soil; the basic breed is the Ongole breed; the terms sambaka and kalam are still used for rice types in southern India; at least 80 plant species, of the 125, exist today in the state of Andhra Pradesh; the technique of transplanting rice was widely practiced in Krishna-Godavari deltas in 100 A. D. (Ayachit–Sadhale–Nene 2002, 146). This last argument is debatable: the age of the technique of transplantation may haven been earlier than Buddha's time (Gombrich 1988, 52). The climatological data of the text are also perplexing: at one place hot season and cold season (316) at another place spring, summer and winter (620) are mentioned. The first roughly correspond to the general division of the meteorological year in India without any specific feature of certain parts of the country. In short, the data are rather heterogeneous and do not allow us to make unanimous conclusions.

The treatise contains 849 verses divided in five main parts or chapters. The first serves as a kind of introduction. The second and third comprise several sub-chapters. Altogether the redaction of the work is very loose. The problems connected with this issue cannot be solved until other manuscripts are found.

The work has been composed in a metrical form and anuṣṭubh is the only form used. About language and style Sadhale rightly observes 'sometimes it is felt, however, that more elaborate meter could have been used to avoid kulakas (clustering of several verses). One verse for one or other thought is an ideal arrangement but in KKS a sentence or a thought-unit often spreads over two or six verses... The language of KKS is very simple and easy, reminding one of the language of Puranas... Normally, clarity, ease, fluency, and simplicity are the characteristics of Kashyapa's language... However, conciseness and precision of expression which are merits of a writer on the subject of science are also missing here. Examples of prolixity and verbosity are in plenty' (Ayachit–Sadhale–Nene 2002, 130–131). All these observations hold good, however, we have to keep in mind the general character of kṛṣiśāstras and particularly should not forget that Kāśyapa was only a traditional author and the work of redaction rather follows folkloristic pattern than the editorship of śāstras in the strict sense of the term.

The first part called, 'The preliminary advice on the subject', provides a proper argumentation for the importance of agriculture in sacred and profane spheres of life. It narrates to us the mythical provenance of the text (verses 1–24).

The second part, called 'The description of the method for cultivating grain, etc.' (verses 25–599), is divided into 13 sub-chapters. The titles are as follows: 1. Introduction; 2. Division of land; 3. Construction of water reservoirs; 4. Construction of canals, wells, etc.; 5. Characteristics of good farmers and village officers; 6. Procurement of tools, implements, and other resources; 7. Plow worship; 8. Worship of bullocks; 9. Characteristics of good cows and bullocks; 10. Season of farming and determining land for rice and pulses; 11. Procurement of seeds; 12. Plowing for sowing seeds; 13. Cultivating procedure for grain crops; 14. Cultivation of pulses and other crops.

The main product is paddy. The first sub-chapter provides a short introduction in the classification of the soils. It is followed by two lengthy chapters on the establishing of an irrigation system. A separate part is devoted to the eulogy of agriculture and characterization of cultivators. The subsequent two chapters describe the tools of agriculture and the plough. The following two chapters deal with the worship of bull-king and with the marks of cows and bulls. One chapter discusses the proper season for grains and the method used to divide the land, and the other describes the ways of collecting various seeds. A following chapter narrates the method of cultivation which is fit for gaining various grains, and the last one does the same concerning the pulses and some other products such as wheat, barley, millet, sugar-cane and cotton trees and so on.

The third part, called 'The description of the cultivation method for vegetables etc.' (verses 600–777), contains a considerable amount of information about producing vegetables and fruits, gardening (upavanavinoda), and forestry. All this is mixed with arthaśāstra-portions highlighting the tasks of the king in organising the distribution of products and collecting taxes. The verses 757–765 curiously present a short discourse about products obtained from mining.

The fourth part (verses 778–819) is called 'The description of rules regarding edible and unedible things'. The contents are mainly based on the instructions of the Mānavadharmaśāstra (ManuSm V, 5–26) and the Vaikhānasasmārtasūtra (VaikhāSmS IX, 15).

The fifth part, called 'The description of the order of offering various oblations' (verses 820–849), gives a rich variety of cakes and sweets. There is the item called jālepika which may indicate a late date of this portion of the work. With few exceptions all the food names look like relatively modern.

Sadhale considers these two chapters as appendices (Ayachit–Sadhale–Nene 2002, 129).

Kṛṣigītā

Lang.: Malayalam

Ed.: – ed. by C. Govinda Wariar. In: BGOML III (1950) No. 1, 89–107; No. 2, 99–112 and Vol. IV. (1951) 99–113. (hereinafter: Wariar 1950) – Pāṭṭukal. Part II. Ed. by Raghavan Pillai. (hereinafter: Raghavan Pillai 1968 Trivandrum 1968, 109–142.

Lit.: Wariar 1950, 89. – Raghavan Pillai 1968, XXI–XXXI. – Padmanabha Menon 1982, 88. – Rahman 1982, 519. – Wojtilla 1982a, 170 – Vijayalakhsmi 1993, 42–43.

The author of the poem called 'The song/poem on agriculture' is unknown but, as Wariar puts it, he 'wields a facile pen and the lines all have a lucid charm and melodious flow. The metre employed in the first three padas is "Pāna" and the fourth is written in the "Thuḷḷal style"' (Wariar 1950, 89). The highest authority whose teaching is expounded is Bhārgava i. e. Paraśurāma, and traditionally the text is said to have been taken from the Keralotpatti (Rahman 1982, 519). Others believe that it is a translation of the Sanskrit work entitled Keralakalpa. (Padmanabha Menon 1982, 88) The age of the composition is uncertain (Wariar 1950, 89). If we take it as a part of the Keralotpatti, it could not be dated from a time before the 17th century. It has been very popular in Kerala. As Padmanabha Menon reported, it was taught in schools in Northern Kerala at the end of the last century and beginning of this century (Padmanabha Menon 1982, 88).

The poem is composed of four chapters (pāda) and comprises altogether 943 lines.

The first chapter (lines 1–222.) starts with a dialogue between Paraśurāma (Bhārgava Rāma) and the brāhmaṇas of Kerala who are eager to learn the agricultural condition of the region. On their request Paraśurāma gives a proper instruction. He speaks of the requisites of agriculture: cowshed, manure pits, ploughs, axes, spades and the cattle. He describes the values of the good agriculturists: they respect the elders, are free from sensuality, abstain from alcoholic drinks, are honest and accountable therefore they have to be paid well. Next comes a list of operations: proper fencing and manuring, dividing the field, removal of weeds, colleting firewood, preparing the soil, collecting seeds and bestowing water resources.

The second chapter (lines 223–379.) provides further instructions. Paraśurāma says that all agricultural work must proceed according to the prescription of the sages. Then the rules of ploughing, sowing and transplanting of the paddy seedlings come. The proper day for sowing must be calculated on an astronomical basis. Some of the enemies of agriculture such as weeds and pests are also enumerated here: The proximity of water is a major factor in determining the quality of the soil.

The third chapter (lines 380–636) deals with miscellaneous topics. Paraśurāma explains the difference between Kerala and other countries. It is followed by special instruction with regard to pepper and arecanut which must be cultivated on high land and paddy which must be grown on low land. The next details concerning paddy cultivation include classification of seeds, preparation of the paddy field, treatment of the seedlings, or the fitting of the ploughshare in the plough, and the regulation of its position in order to carry out effective ploughing and yoking of the oxen. The subsequent lines narrate the cultivation of coconut, jack fruit and palm trees and maintenance of flower gardens and growing chilis. The ending lines contain prescriptions on deep ploughing, hoeing, making pits for trees and instructions on the agricultural calendar. The brāhmaṇas listened to all this and expressed their wish to hear more about the auspicious days, hours for cultivation and the monsoon.

The fourth chapter (lines 637–943) is the continuation of Paraśurāma's teaching. Ploughing and sowing at night are easier and forests should not be destroyed. Then follows an account of the auspicious and inauspicious days for agriculture. At the end we are taught of the defects and virtues of the cattle including bulls and buffaloes. They are characterized according to their tail, spine, horn, hooves, teeth, spots on the skin, nose, shoulders, hair etc. The buffalo and the bull should not be put under the same yoke.

Kṛṣicakraṅṅal

Lang.: Malayalam

Mss.: To my best knowledge there is a single manuscript kept at the Kerala University Oriental Research Library, Trivandrum under the signature Ms 10856 – G.

Ed.: No information.

Lit.: K. V. Sarma 1972, 100. – Wojtilla 1982a, 170–171.

The author of the text is unknown. The lower – limit of its date is the age of the manuscript which cannot be earlier than the eighteenth century (personal communication from Prof. Unni 1977). It is regarded as a text on natural astrology. (K. V. Sarma 1972, 100) It is a collection of meteorological maxims related to agricultural work.

Kṛṣijñānapradīpikā

Lang.: Kanarese

Ed.: AAI 165 (?)

Lit.: AAI 165.

It is a modern treatise based on āgamaśāstras and purāṇas and compiled by a certain Sri Nagabhusonaghans – mathadharya (sic!) who lived between 1826–1884. (AAI 165).

Kṛṣiparāśara

Lang.: Sanskrit

Mss.: Ms Tagore 24, IOL Catalogue No. 6475 ; one manuscript from Cambridge, two manuscripts from the late Central Provinces and Bengal reported by Kielhorn and Rajendralala Mitra and one manuscript from the Provincial Museum Cuttack (all these are recorded in: NCC IV, 284) – The report about the eleven manuscripts from the Orissa State Museum Bhubaneshwar was not available to the editors of NCC while compiling the volume in question. (Mishra 1973, 122–123) – There is also a manuscript kept at the Congress Library, Washington deposited by Eugene Hotaling, former professor of education at Valley City State College in North

Dakota. It is called Kṛṣipaddhati and written in Bengali characters. The manuscript contains some genuine readings that may be of immense help for a new critical edition of the text (Wojtilla 2001a 188–189).

Ed.: Kṛṣisaṁgrahaṁ Pūjyapāda – Parāśaramunipraṇītaṁ... Giricandraśarmaṇā... mudritaṁ. Kālikātā 1862, 1–18. – Vācaspatyam, compiled by Śrī Tāranātha Tarkavāchaspati. Calcutta 1873–1884. Vol. III, 2197–2201 (hereinafter: Vācaspatyam). This text is incomplete: verse 1 (invocation) and verses 10–79 concerning meteorological observations have not been included here. – Ed. by Tārakānta Kāvyatīrtha [= so – called Vaṅgavāsī-edition: Sanskrit–Bengali parallel text] Kālikātā B. S. 1322 [= 1915] R. P. Das raised some doubts about the identity of this text and that of the 1862 edition, but he could not form definite opinion because he could not get access to the Vaṅgavāsī text (Das 1988, 508). It is a pity, that I also have not seen it yet. Ganguly 1930–1931 uses it and translates excerpts from it. – Kṛṣi-Parāśara. Ed. G. Majumdar and S. C. Banerji. Calcutta 1960. (hereinafter: Majumdar–Banerji 1960). It is a critical edition with English translation, introductory study and copious references. It was reviewed by Birwe (Birwe 1964) and Kuiper (Kuiper 1969). This is a reliable text; however, the editors did not take into consideration the texts printed in Calcutta in 1862 (Gopal 1973, 151 note 4). It is a pity, that Gopal wrongly had ascribed the editorship to Prasannakumāra Ṭhākura and so mislead also me while preparing the first edition of the present book. In fact the editor is Giricandra Śarma who followed the intentions of the former (Das 1988, 508). – Kṛṣi-Parāśara. Anuvādak evaṁ prakāśak Caudharī Śrīnārāyaṇa Sinha. Varanasi 1971. (Sanskrit text with Hindi translation. The Sanskrit text is based on the critical edition (hereinafter: Sinha 1971). The edition is valuable for the numerous notes and references to agricultural sayings in Hindi.) – Krishi-Parashara (Agriculture by Parashara) (A text on ancient Indian agriculture in Sanskrit) Translated by Nalini Sadhale. Commentaries by H. V. Balkundi and Y. L. Nene. Secunderabad 1999. (Agri-History Bulletin 2.) (hereinafter: Sadhale–Balkundi–Nene 1999). It was reviewed by Gy. Wojtilla (Wojtilla 2001a) and S. R. Sarma (Sarma 2001).

Transl.: For the Bengali, English and Hindi translations see the respective bilingual editions. There is an English translation by S. Raychaudhuri (1938) – An Oriya translation was published in Cuttack in 1930 (Gopal 1973, 151 note 4) – the text has also a Hungarian translation (Wojtilla 1976).

Lit.: Benthley 1800, 576 (he regarded the text as an insignificant little work and a most palpable forgery) – Majumdar 1927, 207. – Gangopadhyaya 1932 and 1941 – Roy 1948, 30. – Banerji 1955 – De 1960, II. – Birwe 1964 – AAI 154 etc. – Kuiper 1969 – Gopal 1973 (= 1980, 1–30.) – Wojtilla 1976, 1977, 1977a, 1982, 1982a and 1988 – Lal 1980, 126. – Roşu 1986, 258–260. – Das 1988, I and 43; 1997, 205 and 215. – Chowdhury 1992. – Ramdas 1992. – Wojtilla 2001. – Wojtilla 2001a. – Das 2001. – Ayangarya 2003. – Ayangarya 2004.

Parāśara to whom the text has been ascribed, has not been identified. Some scholars take it as a compendium the unknown compilators of which simply followed the intentions of Parāśara (Vācaspatyam 2210). His identification with the author of the Parāśarasmṛti by A. Lal (Lal 1980, 126) and C. S. Sinha (Sinha 1971, 2. – Lal, 1980, 126) is improbable. As Banerji clearly says 'if both Parāśaras are regarded as identical, it becomes difficult to account for the complete absence of verses from the Kṛṣi-parāśara or of any reference to it in the portion of the Parāśara-smṛti dealing with agriculture' (Majumdar–Banerji 1960, vi). He is not the author of a work entitled Vṛkṣāyurveda. (Chowdhury 1992, 33 and Das 1997, 205 and 215). Moreover the authenticity of this latter is not free from doubts (Gopal 1980, 33. – Das 1997, 215). On the other hand there is a reference to a work called kṛṣitantra written by Vṛddhaparāśara in Bhaṭṭotpala's commentary on Arthaśāstra II, 24, 1 (Wojtilla 1997–1998, 676. – Das 1997, 201 note 10). The attribution to Parāśara may be based on the śāstric tradition but as Das rightly remarks such ascriptions are so common in Indian works that as evidence such an ascription is of little value (Das 1997, 205). In this case we may think of the fame of the Parāśara gotra of brāhmaṇas in science, which gave a rank to the work. S. K. De considers the treatise a Sanskrit version of the collective weather – wisdom in the form of popular sayings in vernaculars. In its present form it is a compilation because some verses of it are attributed to Raghunandana to Varāha, Hārīta, Devala, the Rājamārtaṇḍa, the Kṛtyacintāmaṇi and the Devīpurāṇa (De 1960, II). The matter is, however, not as simple since Banerji has already touched this problem and concluded that the borrowing might have taken place vice versa (Banerji 1955, 5). Lallanji Gopal thinks that 'it would not be fair to accuse Parāśara of plagiarism', and it is possible that both Parāśara and Raghunandana used a common source, moreover 'Raghunandana did know the Kṛṣi-Parāśara text' (Gopal 1973, 161).

The text has been variously dated to the 5th century A. D. (Majumdar 1927, 207), to the 6th – 8th centuries (Roy 1948, 30) and to the 6th – 11th centuries (Majumdar–Banerji 1960, VIII–IX). Lallanji Gopal in his meticulous study comes to the conclusion that the middle of the eleventh century is a reasonable date (Gopal 1973, 168). Using the passages ascribed to the Rājamārtaṇḍa, Chowdhury places the composition of the text between c. 950 – 1100 A. D. (Chowdhury 1992, 33). Aufrecht is one of the earliest who recorded of the existence of the work, and stands alone with his opinion according to which the treatise 'although a very modern compilation, is most likely grounded on the ancient Parāśaratantra' (Aufrecht 1869, 26–27).

Most probably the text is of a north-eastern Indian provenance. It is indicated by some desi words such as madikā-/ mayikā- 'a kind of harrow', paccanī- 'goad' which can be connected with Bengali mai- 'a ladder-shaped contrivance used for levelling ricefields' and pāñcan – bāṛi respectively (Kuiper 1969, 215). The manuscript tradition leads us also to Bengal and Orissa. In order to locate the provenance of the text as well as to date it the so-called Hanumān mantra is of great importance. It is inserted in the text after verse 195. The mantra is intended for warding off diseases, insects, birds and beasts being harmful to crops. Having analysed the royal titles attached to god Rāma here Lallanji Gopal convincingly says that the mantra points to north Bengal during the Pāla or early Sena rule (Gopal 1973, 153–154). This incantation is substantially the same in all nanuscripts, but Jyotistattva pp. 689–690 preserved another version. We may call attention to a similar Hanumān mantra in the Vṛkṣāyurveda by Sūrapāla, a text from Bengal from the second half of the eleventh and first half of the twelfth centuries A. D. (Das 1988, 262). The sixteenth-century Viśvavallabha chapter six contains a shorter and slightly different version of the mantra. The same mantra can be found in the eighteenth century Śivatattvaratnākara (ŚivataRaKa VI, 10, 65–67). The author was King Basava, the ruler in a part of the modern Karnataka state. Modern

Bengali almanacs show a close resemblance to the description of the agricultural year presented by the Kṛṣiparāśara (Bhattacharyya 1976, 172). There is no mention of an irrigation system in the text, indicating that it was a territory where the natural rainfall regulates agricultural production. This circumstance points also to the same region. Having taken the termination of the end of the rainy season at the end of August in the text Balkundi places Parāśara in the western parts of the Punjab region along the eastern bank of the Indus river and thinks that he lived in a century earlier than the fourth century B. C. (Sadhale–Balkundi–Nene 1999, 78–79). With regard to the character of the composition of the text and in general that of the similar works in vernaculars I find both the localisation and the dating haphazard.

The text contains 243 verses. C. S. Sinha opines that the extant text is only a portion of a bigger work because the present text deals with the cultivation of paddy only (Sinha 1971, 2). This assumption is not quite unlikely if one compares the work with such texts as the Kāśyapīyakṛṣisūkti. It is noteworthy that the editor of the Kāśyapaśilpa refers to five verses concerning creation (sṛṣṭi) taken from the Parāśarīyakṛṣi on first page of preface to his edition. It is a pity, that these passages cannot be attested in the Kṛṣiparāśara or in any text known to me. At the same time keeping in view its north-eastern Indian provenance where the staple food is paddy this idea can be challenged. Its condition is generally good; however, there are obviously mistakes in certain manuscripts. There is only one lacuna in the text in the Hanumān mantra following the verse 194. As Majumdar and Banerji put it, the book is very easy and affords a pleasant reading; the language is simple, but the variety of metres (anuṣṭubh, indravajrā, upajāti and mālinī) praise the poetic merits of the author (Majumdar–Banerji 1960 xi-xii).

The text which begins with a salutation to Prajāpati and a eulogy of agriculture has been divided in several chapters. According to Majumdar–Banerji they are as follows:

The determination of the Lord (of year)
The determination of the cloud
The ascertainment of āḍhaka of water
The knowledge of rainfall in Pauṣa

The knowledge of rainfall in Māgha
The knowledge of rainfall in Phālguna
The knowledge of rainfall in Caitra
The knowledge of rainfall in Vaiśākha
The indication of rainfall in Jyaiṣṭha
The indication of rainfall in Āṣāḍha
The indication of rainfall in Śrāvaṇa
The knowledge of immediate rainfall
The knowledge of rainfall at the passing of planets
The indication of drought
The supervision of agriculture
The rule about draught-animals
The description of the festival of cows
The procession and entrance of cows
The lifting of cowdung-heap
The description of the constituents of the plough
The ceremony of halarasāraṇa
The rule about the preservation of seeds
The procedure about sowing seeds
The application of the mayikā
The procedure of transplantation
The procedure of the kaṭṭana of paddy
The removal of weeds from paddy
The release of water in Bhādra
The incantation for the cure of the diseases of paddy
The preservation of water
The taking of a handful (of paddy) in Agrahāyaṇa
The planting of medhi in Agrahāyaṇa
The description of (the ceremony called) Puṣyayātrā in Pauṣa
The description of Āḍhaka
The storing of paddy

The contents of the treatise can be summarized thus:

It begins with the praise of agriculture. Since agriculture depends on rainfall a great part is devoted to climatology. These passages stand very near to those in the collection of popular sayings in vernaculars and to those in Sanskrit text on weather-forecast. The next are the rules regulating the treatment of cattle with special emphasis on their role in ploughing. A short instruction concerning manuring forms the next part. It is followed by a very detailed description of the plough (cf. Wojtilla 1977 and 1988). This portion of the text is of great interest from the point of view of technology as well as for the history of language because it abounds in Sanskritised vernacular terms. Prescriptions on the commencement and carrying out of ploughing are dealt with at considerable length. There is enough room for omens and portents connected with this business. The subsequent verses provide detailed instructions on the seeds, sowing, the operations afterwards such as harrowing, transplantation of paddy seedlings, weeding, release of water from the paddy field and magical protection of the seedling from insects and pests which cause harm to crops. Before harvest there is some minor work to be done, such as fixing nala (lit. reed) in the field in order to avert evils to paddy for instance strong wind or simply to scare away mischievous birds, testing the crop by taking a handful of samples (Gangopadhyaya 1932, 65) or for other unknown purposes (Majumdar–Banerji 1960, xvi note; cf. 17 Sadhale–Balkundi–Nene 1999, 91). Earlier we have seen traces of a fertility myth in the mantra following the fixing of reed where nala may symbolise male pole and the paddy field represents the female one (Wojtilla–Wojtilla 1976, 149), however now this assumption appears to me somehow far-fetched. The whole process of cultivation and accordingly the prescriptions of our treatise end with the narrating of the harvest and the connected festival called puṣyayātrā, when the grains of paddy are weighed and stored. The last thing to be done is the Lakṣmīpūjā, the worship of the Goddess of wealth and fortune.

As Majumdar and Banerji justly say, 'the book undoubtedly contains very valuable instructions regarding the important business of agriculture; these instructions, shorn of the superstitious matters, the speculative astronomical observations and the religious practices, cannot fail to impress us even today' (Majumdar–Banerji 1960, XVII). The lasting impact of it can be felt in the practice of Bengali farmers of our time (cf. Bhattacharyya 1976, 171–176).

Kṛṣiviṣaya 'A guide to agriculture' (Law 1918, 276)

Lang.: Sanskrit

Mss.: One manuscript is reported from the private collection of a certain Mahārāja Śrīyukta Satiścandra who lived in Kṛṣṇanagara – Navadvīpa in Bengal. The manuscript is old and accurate (R. Mitra 1871, 379–380).

Ed.: No information

Lit.: R. Mitra 1871 – Law 1918, 276 – Rahman 1982, 519.

The author of this 'Guide to agriculture' in one hundred ślokas as well as the age of the composition is unknown. It deals with various crafts connected with agriculture. As Law rightly observes the first few ślokas quoted in the catalogue by R. Mitra are identical with those of Parāṣaras Krṣisaṁgraha printed at Calcutta (1322 B. S. = 1915) but the last śloka quoted in the same does not coincide with that of the latter (Law 1918, 276).

Kṛṣiśāsana

Lang.: Sanskrit

Ed.: Kṛṣiśāsanaṁ... Daśarathaśāstrisaṁpāditaṁ tatkṛtanārāyaṇabhāṣyarāghavabhāṣyadvyasaṁvalitaṁ... nāgapure prakāśitam. V. S. 1977 (= 1920)

Transl.: Hindi: see above. It is a translation cum commentary.

Lit.: AAI 154. – NCC IV, 284. – Wojtilla 1982a, 167. – Wojtilla 1991 – Wojtilla 1993)

The author is Daśarathaśāstrī, son of Nārāyaṇa, from the Gargagotra of brāhmaṇas who compiled the treatise in the village Śrīsukara (modern Soroṅ in Uttar Pradesh) in 1909. The text was printed in Nagpur in 1920. The book is accounted as a bibliographical rarity. The editors of AAI simply remarked that it was not available to them (AAI 154). One copy in good condition is kept at the India Office Library (= British Library).

The treatise is composed of eleven chapters. Daśarathaśāstrī tells us the details of the editorial work. He thanks those brāhmaṇa friends who know the essence of the soil (bhūmitattva) and who are devoted to the worship of Viṣṇu. In the introduction to the work the author says that among others he used the text of the Kṛṣipaddhati and Kṛṣisaṁgraha, Bṛhatparāśarasmṛti and a work by Cakrapāṇi. What is astonishing is that he borrowed the description of the plough from the later one and was able to make proper emendations where the reading of the Jībānanda Vidyāsāgara edition is in error (Wojtilla 1993, 530–531). There are remains of borrowings from vernaculars: vakṣara – 'plough used for levelling' (VII, 73) is a Sanskritised form of bakhar-/ vakhar while ḍuṇḍi- and ḍoḍaka (ibid.) occur in original form. There are two commentaries, one in Sanskrit and one in Hindi. The Sanskrit commentary is based on not less than fifty sources, including some little known and still unpublished texts such as the Karmalocana, Bhojanakalpataru and the Saṁvatsarapradīpa. The authorities referred to are the Parāśaras, Atri, Nārada, Pṛthu and Marīci. A sketch of the plough according to Pṛthu has been appended to the text; however, we have not located a description for a description. The Parāśaras need no introduction and the role of the mythical king Pṛthu, the cultural hero who invented agriculture, is also well known from the epic tradition. Marīci and Atri made themselves a good name in the Vaikhānasa tradition. The relation of this tradition to agriculture in southern India has been already touched upon. Marīci's name in connection with agriculture can only be attested to in the Liṅgapurāṇa (LiṅgaP I, 5, 40). The reference to Nārada as the authority of the fluctuation of prices is very interesting. A closer examination of it shows that a great deal was borrowed from the Mayūracitraka, which is basically a text on climatology and one manuscript of which has come down to us under the authorship of Nārada. It is a pity that Daśarathaśāstri, who did not forget to refer to the place of the Liṅgapurāṇa, here remains silent. The chapter has resemblances to the respective parts of Hindi Pañcāṅgis and Jantris (cf. Wojtilla 1995, 529). In classical Sanskrit literature we can trace only the short chapter called Arghakāṇḍādhyāya ('The fluctuation of prices') of Varāhamihira's Bṛhatsaṁhitā (BṛSaṁ ch. 412).

The Kṛṣiśāsana is a kṛṣiśāstra in the broadest sense of the term including long chapters on topics that in the narrower sense do not form part of kṛṣiśāstra. With his work the author has had two aims: it is a kṛṣimāhātmya (eulogy of agriculture) and also a dharmarahasya (the secret of dharma intented for cultivators). The titles of the chapters aptly illustrate their contents. They are as follows.

1. The description of the duties of the brāhmaṇas in agriculture. It is a kind of law-book embracing the tradition beginning from the Vedas. In the spirit of the Parāśaras Daśarathaśāstri permits agriculture as a profession for brāhmaṇas.

2. The description of the first foot (pāda) of agriculture. The chapter informs us about the different types of soil and how to make them fertile with help of manuring. It gives room to short hymns and incantations applied in worship of the Earth personified.

3. The description of the marks of bulls. It gives the conventional classification of bulls which follows the varṇa pattern.

4. The description of the medical treatment of bulls. It is an independent work on veterinary science.

5. The description of the foot called the seed.

6. The description of the fourth foot of agriculture called the husbandmen. It discusses the social and health conditions of husbandmen. Practical advice on how to cure diseases can also be read here.

7. The description of the agricultural work. It is a systematic account of examination of the soil, the seeds, ploughing, sowing and the implements used for these purposes.

8. The description of the knowledge of rainfall. It proceeds on the footsteps of Parāśara and provides us the necessary knowledge of climatology.

9. The description of the ordinary and the high prices of items. It is an account of the seasonal fluctuation of prices of various agricultural products.

10. The description of agricultural work beginning with weeding.

11. The definition of laws concerning agriculture. It comprises the sacred law explaining how to perform sacrifices and worship.

Kṛṣiśāstra or *Kṛṣisamayanirṇaya*

Lang.: Sanskrit

Mss.: There is a single manuscript kept at the Government Oriental Manuscript Library, Chennai (Madras) under the signature MS No. 5276. The manuscript itself is a transcript in easily readable Devanāgarī characters made by a certain Nīlakaṇṭha Nambūdripād inhabitant of Kaññūr-mana, Ottapalam, District Malabar in 1926–1927. The material is paper, and the number of leaves is 16 (= 32 pages). Ottapalam is situated in the vicinity of Palghāt tāluq (district) in Central Kerala. Kaññūr-mana means Kaññūr-house where mana indicates the abode of a brāhmaṇa while Kaññūr refers to the house of Nīlakaṇṭha Nambūdripād. There are 20 lines on each page. In spite of considerable efforts in the past five years I was unable to trace the original manuscript either in Chennai (Madras) or in Kerala. The copy is incomplete therefore the title is also ambiguous. The first verse clearly states the aims of the unknown author:

athātaṁ sampravakṣyāmi saṁkīrṇaviṣaye nṛṇām
kriyāṇāmapi satkālaṁmuhūrtañcaviśeṣataṁ

'Now I shall declare the proper time and especially the moment with regard of various things for men and also for activities.'

Ed.: Kṛṣi – Parāśara Ed. by G. P. Majumdar and S. C. Banerji. Calcutta 1960. Appendix. AAI 160 wrongly gives No 5278 (cf. Majumdar–Banerji iii; NCC IV, 284; Das 1988, 43–44). The learned editors did not undertake the job of textual criticism, and because they found the text 'hopelessly corrupt', they did not venture to make 'hazard emendations', but reproduced the text unaltered, indicating the 'absolutely unintelligible' portions with dots. They are perfectly right so far as the text abounds in orthographical and grammatical errors. For to me unknown reasons they fully left out the verses from 236 to 294.

Lit.: Menon 1903, 99. – AAI 160 – NCC IV, 284. – Wojtilla 1982a, 168. – Das 1988, 43–44.

The text containing 294 – in the manuscript unnumbered – verses mostly in anuṣṭubh metre is written in poor Sanskrit, because of a scribe's carelessness, it abounds in orthographical and grammatical errors. There are only two lacunas in the text (verses 18b and 92ab). Other peculiarities of the manuscript are as follows: cancellation of akṣaras (verses 6a, 63a and 277a), deletion of inserted lines between the verses 14b-15a and 186ab, corrections (verses 4b, 74c, 77c, 81a, 111ab, 149a and 211a) and insertion of akṣaras (148b).

Its language is poor Sanskrit. Notwithstanding it shows up some literary merits at least what the variety of metres employed in the treatise are concerned. The used metres are as follows: indravajra (verses 71–72), rathoddhatā (verse 106), sragdharā (verse 90), upajāti (verses 75–76, 135–136 and 158–159) and vasantatilakā (verses 89 and 109) while the remaning ones are composed in anuṣṭubh. As to authorship and date of composition we are in full darkness. On the ground of the existing long tradition of natural astronomy in Kerala we might conclude that it was written well before the eighteenth century. The provenance of the work is clear: the single extant manuscript and certain points of the contents confirm this assumption. In Ottapalam tāluq on the bank of river Perār a grāmakṣetra of Panniyūr i. e. a brāhmaṇa settlement is recorded (Veluthal 1978, 24). Palghāt tāluq (district) has been regarded a place where the most orthodox forms of agricultural ceremonies including their astronomical aspects are prevalent (Menon 1903, 99). The flora and fauna described in the compendium further underlines this assumption. There are typical products of Kerala such as nālikera 'cocos nucifera' (verses 266, 271, 272 and 278), nāgalatā 'piper betle' (verse 256), pūga 'betel-nut tree', 'areca catechu' (verses 57, 60, 258 and 259), tāmbūla 'piper betle' (verses 58 and 254). The way of cultivating nālikera is a recurring topic in more than one chapter and it can be compared with the relevant parts of the Kṛṣigītā and is well in harmony with the present-day circumstance in the Ottapalam district (Bhatt 1997, 824–825). Elephants gaja (verses 142, 212, 247 and 285) or karin (verse 216) play very important role in everyday life. It should not be forgotten than the single extant Sanskrit textbook on elephant-lore the Mātaṅga-līlā is very much popular in Kerala (Edgerton 1931, vii). There are references to forest-clearing (verse 8) and the wood has been used for constructing houses. The so-called slash-and-burn type of cultivation has been also indicated (verse 17). Both phenomena are common in Kerala. The extant text is of an encyclopedical character. The treatise in its extant form divides itself into thirteen chapters.

1. The precepts of cultivation.
2. The precepts of sowing.
3. The yogas for taking earth. (There are verses bearing on planting, watering, domestic rites and settling boundary disputes.)
4. The yogas making friends.
5. The yogas for making quarrel.
6. The yogas for collecting wealth and grain.
7. The duties concerning the material goods of the village(?)
8. The yogas for killing diseases.
9. The yogas for medical attendance of diseases. (Here some serious diseases are mentioned such as guhyaroga 'the diseases of the pudenda' verse 161; kuṣṭa 'leprosy' verse 166; apasmāraroga 'epilepsy' verse 172. The means of remedy are mantras and herbal medicines verse 172.)
10. The precepts of protection against tree diseases, damages of wells and reseroirs, (of protection) of grain.
11. The precepts of strengthening pillars and gardens at the building of a house and that of horses, cows and the churning milk into butter.
12. The precepts of buying, selling, all [kinds] of reservoirs and the like.
13. Unknown title. (Here the manuscript abruptly ends and the colophon together with title is missing. According to its contents it may be even the continuation of the former chapter).

To sum up the text is a kṛṣiśāstra in the sense of the loosely edited collections of agricultural sayings in vernaculars with a great deal of contents rather to dharmaśāstra or arthaśāstra. The main object of the work is to teach how to choose the proper time and season for agricultural activities, horticulture and the works essential in everyday life.

Kedārakalpa

Lang.: Sanskrit

Ed.: No information

Lit.: Das 1988, 3.

The work is mentioned in the Bengali foreword to Upavanavinoda (Das 1988, 3). It is unlikely that the text is identical with any of the sections of the Skandapurāṇa (cf. pw II, 98 and MW 309) or of the Nandipurāṇa (cf. MW 309) bearing the same title.

Keralakṛṣi

Lang.: Sanskrit

Mss.: A palm-leave manuscript is kept at the Mackenzie collection. As to the manuscripts of Keralotpatti see NCC V, 19.

Ed. transl.: no information.

Lit.: Wilson 1828^2, 362 and 347.

It is an account of the cultivation of the lands in Malabar from the Keralotpatti (Wilson 1828^2, 362). The latter is a general account of the province or Kerala or Malabar. The composition is ascribed to Śaṅkara ācārya and the original of some portion of it may have been his work, but a great part is of a much more recent period as it notices even the coming of the Portuguese (Wilson 1828^2, 347).

Keralakalpa

Lang.: Malayalam

Mss.: Several cf. Padmanabha Menon 1982, 88.

Ed. transl.: No information.

Lit.: Padmanabha Menon 1982, 88.

According to Padmanabha Menon it is a poem in Malayalam which is said to be a translation of a Sanskrit work on agriculture believe to have been compiled by Paraśurāma for the benefit of his people in Kerala. In rural parts of Malabar, especially in the north, the poem is taught in village schools, and the methods of cultivation now practised by the agricultural classes are mostly in accordance with the precepts laid down in this poem. It starts with meteorological forecast based on astronomical observations (ibidem). The selection of land for cultivation must be made with utmost care and they must be fenced and richly manured, ploughed not less than six times (op. cit. 90–92). It prescribes three kinds of paddy cultivation: dry seed cultivation, sprouted cultivation and transplanted cultivation (op. cit. 95–96). The agricultural year begins on the first of Meṭam (April–May) and the village astrologer or kaṇiyān is consulted to fix an auspicious day for the turning of the first sod of the season (op. cit. 98). The text speaks of the harvest of the second crop of the year in Makara (January–February) (op. cit. 99).

Kṣetratattva

Lang.: Sanskrit

Ed.: No information.

Lit.: Das 1988, 3.

The work is mentioned in the Bengali foreword to Upavanavinoda (Das 1988, 3).

Kṣetraprakāśa

Lang.: Sanskrit

Mss.: No information. Neither CC nor NCC record it. Ed.: No information. Lit.: Law 1918, 279. – Sarkar 1937, 438.

According to B. K. Sarkar it was once printed (Sarkar 1937, 438). No details of the publication have been given.

Khanār – bocan

Lang.: Bengali

Mss.: CCBM I, 42.

Ed.: It is not possible here to give a complete survey of the editions; therefore, we shall only recall the oldest and more important ones. Khanār vachana. The astrological sayings of Khanā. Golachipa 1875 – Khanār vacan. Ed. by P. S. Bhattacharya Calcutta B. S. 1315 (= 1908) – Khanār vachana ed. by Saracchandra Śīla. Calcutta 1915 – S. K. De: Bānglā Pravād. Calcutta B. S. 1359 (= 1952) Varāhamihira – Khanā Jyotiṣ granth [ed. by]

Śrī Kālimohan Vidyāratna Kartṛk. Kālikātā [undated] Sulabh Kālikātā Lāibreri pp. 202–224. (hitherto: Kartṛk) – Excerpts have been published in: Majumdar–Banerji 1960 passim.

Transl.: To our best knowledge there is not any complete translation of it into foreign languages. There are excerpts from it in English (Chakravarti 1930, 374–376 and Das Gupta 1935, passim.: a great number of sayings together with the Bengali original) and in Russian (Novikova 1965, 27–29).

Lit.: Rāya 1903 – Chatterji 1926, 131–132. – Chaudhuri 1935, 7. – Roy 1948, 25. – Sen 1949, 52–57. – Sen Gupta 1955, 59–61. – Banerji 1955, 32. – AAI 158. – Sircar 1965, 25. – Tripathi 1971, 7. – Wojtilla 1982a, 169.

Khanā, the traditional author of this collection of sayings was an astrologer. She was the wife of Mihira, son of Varāha (Roy 1948, 29; Sen Gupta 1955, 59–61). Some scholars translate the name as 'learned man' and derive it from the Tibetan cmkhan- (Chaudhuri 1935, 7) or regard it as a vernacular form from a Sanskrit kṣaṇada – 'astrologer' (Sircar 1965, 25).

The text has been variously dated from the 8th century (Sen 1949, 52–53) to the period after 1400 (Chatterji 1926, 131–132). The core of the text might have been composed by a relatively early writer, however, the extant text abounds in later interpolations (Banerji 1955, 32). The occurrence of such plant names as tambāku- 'tobacco' introduced by the Portuguese to India probably around 1605 (Gazetter III, 49) and ālū 'potato' denoting plants of American origin – certainly belong to these loci.

The existence of a Marathi version (Tripathi 1971, 7) may speak for the great popularity of the work outside of Bengal. It might have been made in a period when Maratha's political power was present in North-eastern India in the first half of the eighteenth century.

The sayings of the collection are concerned with climatic conditions, agricultural operations and the like (Banerji 1955, 32). The collection published by Kartṛk touches among others the following topics: auspicious and inauspicious omens of the year; calculating storms and rainfall; success of paddy; methods of growing grains; cutting grains; proverbs concerning radish, betel, tobacco etc. From another versions let me take some sayings: 'He who cultivates the soil in the days of the full moon and the new moon is sure to suffer misery. His cows suffer from rheumatism, and scarcity prevails in his house' (Dasgupta 1935, 225). 'The peasants are to start for the fields on an auspicious day. There should be no inauspicious things to be seen on the way. Just reaching the field they have to enter it by the eastern side and begin ploughing from thence' (Dasgupta 1935, 228). 'Khanā says to the cultivator that if fleecy clouds be followed by wind in the full-moon day of the month of Kārtik, winter crops grow plentifully; but if there be cloud and rain in he night, it is fruitless to go to the field (i. e., to expect any harvest)' (Ganguly 1930, 744). 'The year in which it rains in the 9th day of the full-moon in the month of Āṣāḍh, the heron will walk over the very bed of the sea. If it drizzles on that day, it will be followed by heavy showers throughout the year to the extent of making fish inhabit the top of mountains (i. e., the earth will be flooded). If it rains now and then, there will be a rich harvest and if the sun sets under a clear cloudless horizon, the crops will not grow at all' (Ganguly 1930, 744–745). The comparison of the existing printed texts, different versions and the preparation of a critical edition are badly needed. A proper analysis of the contents can be made only after that.

Gurusaṁhitā

Lang.: Sanskrit

Mss.: There is a single manuscript (No. 34725) in the Sarasvati Bhavan Library of the Sampurnanand Sanskrit University, Varanasi. It contains 61 sheets of the size 6" x 8.2".

Ed.: The Gurusaṁhitā. An ancient text on weather-forecasting by Lallanji Gopal. Banaras 1981.

Transl.: No information.

Lit.: Gopal 1981. – Wojtilla 1982a, 167. – Gopal 1983. – Gopal 1984. – Das 1988, 8.

The text is bearing on meteorology and also climatology in 492 verses. Investigating the indications on the nature of rainfall the author also tackles its effects in agricultural production. In certain verses practical advices are given as to preservation and hoarding of crops (Gopal 1981, 47). The work can be dated from the end of the twelfth century – beginning of the thirteenth century A. D. (Gopal 1981, 45).

Ghāgh aur Bhaḍḍarī kī kahāvateṅ

Lang.: Hindi, Gujarati, Marathi and Rajasthani

Mss.: The earliest extant manuscript of the sayings of Bhaḍḍarī dates from 1373 and belongs to an astrological work: Svādhyāya saṁgraha pustikā by Lokohitācārya (Datta 1988, 1383).

Ed.: Here it is not possible to give a complete survey of the editions. I shall recall only the oldest or the most important ones. Ghāgh aur Bhaḍḍarī. Saṁpādak Rāmnareś Tripāṭhi. [Prayāg] 1949[2] – Saṁpādak Paṇḍit Rāmalagna Pāṇḍeya, Vārāṇasī [undated] – Śakunāvalī. Astrological and other omens and auguries by Bhaddalī. Agra 1868 and its reprints (Hindi) – Bhaḍalī – vākya. The astrological maxims of Bhaḍalī, the daughter of Hudaḍ, a Brahman of Marwar. Ed. with introduction by Harajīvana Purushottama Śukla. Nadiad 1882 (Gujarati) – Sahadeva Bhāḍalī. (According to Laping 1979, 44 note 4: Marathi) – Some verses of the Rajasthani version have been published in magazines and journals (Datta 1988, 1384). There are ca. 150 sayings in the edition of the Kṛṣiparāśara edited by Caudharī Śrīnārāyaṇa Sinha (cf. Kṛṣiparāśara).

Transl.: Grierson 1885, 274–278 English, excerpts)

Lit.: Christian 1891, 204. – Tivari 1946 – R. N. Tripathi 1949, 19–20, 1952, 12. – AAI 158 – Sircar 1965 – Tripathi 1971 – Laping 1979, 44. – Wojtilla 1982a, 169. – Datta 1988, 1383–1384.

Ghāgh's name is often interchanged with that of Ḍāk and the same also happens with Bhaḍḍarī. Nothing is known about his personality. The name most likely means 'clever', 'cunning', 'experienced'. Bhaḍḍarī, Bhaḍḍalī or Bhaṇḍarī is regarded as Ghāgh's wife by the Jaina author of the Meghamālā Bhaḍḍalīvākya composed in Rajasthan in 1674 (Datta 1988, 1383). R. N. Tripathi says that

Ghāgh was a Dube brāhmaṇa, who lived in the village called Caudharī Sarāy in the vicinity of Kanauj and enjoyed a great reputation in the court of Akbar (1556–1605) (R. N. Tripathi 1949, 19–20). Sircar thinks that the name Ghāgh is a common noun which simply means 'old, wise man', while the name Bhaḍḍarī refers to a community of astrologers called bhadlī or bhadalī in Rajasthan, bhaduri, bhaddari or bhadri in Uttar Pradesh (Sircar 1965, 26). Christian speaks of a certain Bhaddar who was a man and poet whose 'descendants (an inferior class of Brahmans) are still supposed to reside in a village of the Shahabad district [in Bihar]' (Christian 1891, 204).

The age of the oldest manuscripts roughly determines the date of the sayings of Bhaḍḍarī. As to the sayings of Ghāgh, we do not have any fixed point. Tripathi is right when he says that the collection has manifoldly been transformed and reshaped by villagers of different parts of North India according to their tongue. Consequently the birth-place of Ghāgh cannot be traced on the ground of the language of the variants (Tripathi 1949, 19). I think that presence of basic Arabic-Persian terms referring to agriculture such as kharīf and rabī point to a period not earlier than the time when Hindusthani was in the making or rather to the age of Akbar (cf. Chatterji 1960^2, 199) maintained also by the tradition discussed.

The edition by Paṇḍit Rāmalagna Pāṇḍeya contains 399 verses under the name of Ghāgh and 249 attributed to Bhaḍḍarī respectively. The main topics touched upon in the sayings are as follows: the day for sowing grains; method of sowing; millet field; horse-bean field; crops which is reaped in the month Bhādrapadā; barley field; gram field; sugar-cane; sowing rabī crops; sowing wheat; weeding and hoeing; field for cereals and pulses; land production; manuring; time for ploughing; harrowing; fields fit for kharīf crops and paddy; rice plants which on being sown are transplanted to another field; species of paddy; preparation of the soil; setting up nursery; sprinkling water; reaping; grain diseases; paddy field arranged according to the 'Japanese method'; using water in the field and in irrigation; the water requirement of different crops; rules of watering in detail; ploughing and hoeing; the eulogy of the field; the usage of plough and oxen; comparison of the traditional (deśī) plough and the modernised one; the Hariyana bull; knowledge of bulls; methods of protecting crops in unfavourable season; millet and maize; the duties of a good framer; buffaloes; planning diet according to season and month; vegetables etc.

In order to illustrate the way of expression in these sayings here are the English renderings of three maxims taken from different versions. 'Plough little, harrow much, and have your field boundaries high. If what should come does not then do so, you can abuse Ghāgh' (Grierson 1885, 174). 'If you see a cloudless night and a cloudy day, be sure, says Ghāgh, that the rains are at end' (Christian 1891, 221). A comparison of the printed versions and further collection of variants in the Hindi language belt is still a desideratum.

Cāṣāpālā

Lang.: Bengali

Ms.: Calcutta University Ms No 2455.

Ed.: No information

Transl.: Das Gupta 1935 (excerpts in English)

Lit.: Das Gupta 1935, 229, 264–265.

The author Rāmeśvar Bhaṭṭācārya who is also the author of a poem called Śiva-saṅkīrtan composed in 1710. He is a keen observer of the life of the agrarian population in South-west Bengal which had been always a purely rice-producing area. He shows an unpretended sympathy for the poor. As Sen puts it his poem is 'one of the best of the century if not the best' (Sukumar Sen, 1960, 151). The Cāṣāpālā (lit. 'The ploughman's turn') presents a vivid, though rather exaggerated description of the making of various agricultural implements such as ploughs, ladders, rice-husking pedals, and the first-tilling ceremony the living condition of agriculturists. An interesting passage from the text reads thus: 'It is with great trouble that harvest can be gathered. If there is drought then it is all over with the peasant. If there is good crop forthcoming in any one year, the king is cruel enough to put it to sale for his own benefit at the expense of the poor cultivators. In spite of the good harvest it is not the cultivators who really get the profit – but the king. The peasants till the soil amidst immense sufferings in the mud and bog, and drag on their miserable existence not so much by mixing the really good men as by coaxing very bad people who are selfseeking to the extreme and are the real masters of the land' (Cāṣāpālā manuscript fol. 3.: Das Gupta 1935, 264).

Jyotistattva

Lang.: Sanskrit

Ed.: – by Jībananda Vidyāsāgara Calcutta 1895.

Transl.: No information.

Being a chapter of Smṛtitattva of Raghunandana, flourished between 1500–1600, Jyotistattva yields a good information about agriculture, although it is, 'in most cases, a repetition of the work of Parāśara couched in a different language' and it does not show any material improvement on the former so far as the practical agricultural problems are concerned (Banerji 1955, 31). Curiously it contains on pages 689–690 an another version of the Hanumān mantra which otherwise is substantially the same with minor variations in all the versions (Majumdar–Banerji 1960, 48, note to line 6).

Ḍāker bocan

Lang.: Assamese, Bengali, Maithili, Rajasthani.

Mss.: According to Basak there are twelfth century manuscripts of the Old-Bengali version in manuscript collections in Nepal (Basak 1969, XXVI). Some manuscripts of the Maithili version are kept at the S. S. Sanskrit University Library in Darbhanga (Datta 1987, 834).

Ed.: It is not possible to give a complete survey of the editions. We shall only recall the oldest or more important ones. Ḍāk-bhaṇitā. Verses embodying ethical precepts, agricultural maxims, fortune-telling based on the study of physiognomy and astrology and like by Ḍāk. Revised and edited by Yajñarāma Dāsa, Calcutta 1885 (Assamese) – S. K. De: Bāṅglā

Pravād. Calcutta B. S. 1359 (=1952) (Bengali) – Jagdish Singh Gahlot: Rājasthānī krishikahā Vateṁ [sic!] (Rajasthani).

Transl.: To our best knowledge there is not any full translation of it into foreign languages. There are excerpts from the Bengali in English (Grierson 1885, 274, 276 and 280) and in Russian (Novikova 1965, 10–18) – some Maithili sayings in Christian 1891. – few Rajasthani sayings in Sircar 1965, 26–27.

Lit.: Carnegy 1853 (to our knowledge the first report on the sayings in English). – Ghosa 1908 – Chatterji 1926, 131–132. – Chakravarti 1930, 377. – Barua 1933, 189 and 319–320. – Sen 1949, 52–57. – Choudhury 1959, 395–396. – De 1960, II. – Sircar 1965 – Basak 1969, XXVI. – Tripathi 1971, 7. – Choudhary 1971, 235. – Wojtilla 1982, 168. – Datta 1987, 834.

Traditionally the collection is ascribed to a single person called Ḍāka(a) who lived in Assam in the village of Lehidangara (Chakravarti 1930, 311). Barua also identifies him as an inhabitant of the village Lehidangara in the ninth century (Barua 1933, 189 and 319–320). Sircar believes that the sayings were originally assigned to a single astrologer, and later divided between two, Ḍāk and Khanā. The Bengali collection reflects this later development, while the Assamese and Maithili collections attribute all the verses to Ḍāk (Sircar 1965, 24). Verses of Ḍāk have been known as those of Ghāgh in Uttar Pradesh (Sircar 1965, 25) and since his name occurs as Ḍāṅk in Rajasthan, this collection was probably very popular in Northern India. According to the Rajasthani tradition 'Ḍāk (Ḍāṅk) was a brāhmaṇa who flourished in the age of king Parīkṣita of the Mahābhārata. He was a sound mathematician and astrologer and was the husband of Sāvitrī, daughter of the great physician Dhanvantari. Another name of their Sāvitrī was Bhaḍli who was herself a great astrologer' (Sircar 1965, 26).

So it is clear that different persons and traditions have been intermingled in the collection under the name of Ḍāk. Even as to the Bengali or Assamese collection it is difficult to say whether it is the composition of a single individual (Datta 1987, 834). Sircar thinks that the word simply means 'announcing' and so the alternative Bengali form of the author's name Ḍākpuruṣa means 'an announcer of proclamations' (Sircar 1965, 25).

It can be assumed that the core of the collection belongs to the early medieval times in a period when the Assamese and Bengali had not yet been divided into two distinct languages. Sen dates the Bengali version between 800–1200 A. D. (Sen 1949, 52–57). De is of the opinion that some verses might have been translated into Sanskrit and incorporated in the Kṛṣiparāśara (De 1960, II). On linguistic grounds Chatterji dates the extant Bengali text in a period after 1400 (Chatterji 1926, 131–132).

This oldest collection of agricultural sayings in the vernacular covers a wide range of practical knowledge concerning climatology and the routine of cultivation. A typical saying reads thus: 'If it rains in the month of Phāgun, urid is spoilt; if in the month of Chait, lemons; if in the asterism of Krittika, the toddy palms; and if in that of Swāti, beans and sesamum, saith Dāk, the Gowāla' (Grierson 1885, 275). Let here stand examples from the Rajasthani version. 'Dank says. If the sky is thickly clouded during the whole month of Posh but it is cloudless in the bright half of Chait, O Bhaḍli grain will sell cheaper than a maund per Rupee.' 'Ḍank says to Bhaḍḍalī, clouds flying in the morning and cold winds blowing in the evening are sure signs of famine' (Sircar 1965, 26–27). 'If Mirgsira (in June) is hot, Rohini (about beginning of June) rains, and Aradra (middle of June) gives a few drops, saith Dāk hear, O Bhillari, (rice will be so plentiful that) even dogs will turn up their noses at it' (Christian 1891, 209). The most urgent task would be a critical edition which collated the printed text and the individual sayings in other works. It may serve as a solid basis for the whole history of kṛṣiśāstra as a branch of science. The edition would be an important contribution to literature as well.

Tirukkaivalakkam

Lang.: Tamil

Ed.: Ēreḻupatu 1886 – Mahākavi Kampar iyaṟṟiya. Tirukkaivalakkam. Ceṇṇai 1969 – Kopālakirusṇāmācāriyar. Kampeṇi 1969.

Lit.: Zvelebil 1975, 185. – Wojtilla 1982a, 170.

It is a spurious work in praise of agriculture (Zvelebil 1975, 185).

Nuskha dar fann - i - falāhat

Lang.: Persian

Mss.: Two manuscripts of it are known to us. One is kept at the India Office Library (= British Library) (CPM No 2791) and contains 37 fols and 13 illustrations. There is a summarized version of the text in the Āzād Library at the Aligarh Muslim University: Ms 51 Lytton Collection. It was transcribed in the year 1693 (Rahman 1990, 62 note 7). Ed. transl.: Nuskha Dar Fanni-Falahat ('The art of agriculture') (Persian manuscript compiled in the 17th century by the Mughal Prince Dara Shikoh). Translated by Razia Akbar, commentaries by K. L. Mehra, K. L. Chadha, J. S. Kanwar and Y. L. Nene. Secunderabad 2000 (Agri-History Bulletin 3.). (hereinafter: Akbar–Mehra–Chadha–Kanwar–Nene 2000). This edition is based on Ms 51 Lytton.

Lit.: CPMOIL – Rahman 1982, 39 and 62.

The work has been traditionally attributed to prince Dārā Shukoh (at Rahman 1982 and at Akbar–Mehra–Chadha–Kanwar–Nene 2000 stands Shikon), but it appears to be that of Amānullah Husaini, son of Mahābat Khān, a noble in the court of Jahangir (1605–1627) (Rahman 1990, 39).

The literary translation of the title is 'Inventory of the art of agriculture'. According to Rahman it is a tract on agriculture forming the eleventh amal of a larger anonymous work with a few marginal notes. It gives a considerable amount of information about crops, vegetables, fruits, trees, herbs, about the preparation of the soil and harvesting techniques and about the time of harvesting, as well as practical information needed for improving the yield. An interesting feature is the use of astronomical knowledge in planting and harvesting. Cotton cultivation occupies an important part in the work. However, the text is mostly devoted to gardening practices (Rahman 1982, 39). The colophone of the printed text reads thus: This book 'The inventory art of Agriculture' written in the month of Zelqadha 1207 hijri copied from the book Ganj-e-Badawar compiled by Dara Shikoh in which the science of medicine, etc. is also mentioned. The Persian text does not have paragraph numbers. For practical reasons in the English translation the paragraphs have been numbered: there are 305 paragraphs. As Mehra highlights the work provides information and recommendations for undertaking cultivation of economic plants in both 'dry-lands' and 'wet-lands', and in different seasons and agroclimatic conditions. The text refers to about 100 plant species (Akbar–Mehra–Chadha–Kanwar–Nene 2002, 47). Certain horticultural practices deserve scientific scrutiny or require verification. Interesting examples are the paragraphs dealing with the transplantation of big tree (11–15), the techniques recommended for obtaining seedless pomegranate and avoiding cracking in pomegranate fruits (19–20) or grafting (22–25). Kanwar remarks that the text is neither an exhaustive manual nor a treatise based on any well-planned research as we understand today, but the advisors of Dārā Shikoh had probably travelled widely in Central Asia, Iran, Turkey and northern India and collected information from various sources including field-crop farmers, fruit and vegetable growers, and users of herbs and medical plants (Akbar–Mehra–Chadha–Kanwar–Nene 2002, 62). Having compared the number of paragraphs under each plant species Nene makes an interesting conclusion: the person(s) from who Dārā shikoh obtained information had far more experience in West Asia/ Mediterranean regions than in the Indian subcontinent (Akbar–Mehra–Chadha–Kanwar–Nene 2000, 68).

Pairu Maḍava Vivaraṇamu

Lang.: Telugu

Mss.: According to AAI 164 Pairu Madava Vivara [sic!] 'it is a copy of an old manuscript on the mode of cultivation'. The signature of the transcript is 363|163. It is a pity that the name of the library or collection is not mentioned.

Ed. trans.: No information.

The title 'A detailed account of small opening of channels into fields (maḍava) and growing crops' indicates its subject.
Lit.: AAI 164.

Meghamālā

Mss.: Sarasvati Bhavan Library, Varanasi under the signatures: 34 544, 34 545, 35 198, 35 328, 35 728, 37 202 and 37 334.

Ed. transl.: No information. Verses 1–44 of Ms 37 202 are printed in Tripathi 1971. 150–153.

Lit.: Tripathi 1971, 150–153. – Gopal 1981, 23–25. – Pingree 1981, 71. – Datta 1988, 1383.

The text of which there are seven manuscripts deals with meteorological predictions, particularly of rains can probably be dated from the sixth-ninth centuries A. D. (Gopal 1981, 24). According to Pingree there are different works under this title: one is ascribed to Garga and another to Śiva (Pingree 1981, 71). Curiously a Rajasthani (?) manuscript is kept at the Anūpa Sanskrit Library, Bikaner with the name Meghamālā Bhaḍḍalīvākya written by a Jain scholar in 1674 (Datta 1988, 1383).

Lokavijaya-yantra

Lang.: Prakrit

Ed. transl.: Lokavijaya-yantra saṁpādaka Nemicandra Śāstrī. Vārāṇasī Vīra nirvāṇa saṁvat 2497 (=1969).

According to the editor it is earlier than the Bṛhatsaṁhitā of Varāhamihira (sixth century A. D.). At any rate it is earlier than the Rayaṇaparikkhā (CCDPL XXXI) written by Thakkura Pherū in 1315 (Sarma 1984, 3). In 30 verses it deals with the influence of rain on agricultural operations. Verses 9, 10, 14, 17, 18, 22 and 27 are especially instructive.

Vatsaraphala

Lang.: Sanskrit

Mss.: Oppert 1880, No. 6190.

Ed. transl.: No information.

It is a text of unknown date and author bearing on the various products of the year.

Vanamālā

Lang.: Sanskrit

Mss.: According to AAI 160–161 one manuscript was recorded in the Catalogue of the Mithila Institute of Research and Post-graduate Studies in Sanskrit, Darbhanga under the signature 328, but Dr R. K. Kak could not trace it on the spot.

Ed.: Some excerpts are printed in Tripathi 1971, passim.

Transl.: No information.

Lit.: AAI 160–161. – Tripathi 1971, 76.

The author is a certain Jīvanātha from Mithila (Tripathi 1971, 76) and the text deals with meteorological phenomena closely connected with agricultural production.

Varṣalakṣaṇa

Lang.: Malayalam – Sanskrit

Mss.: There is a manuscript under the signature 6914A at the Library of the Oriental Research Institute, Kerala University, Trivandrum.

Ed. Transl.: No information.

Lit.: K. V. Sarma, 1972, 164. – Wojtilla 1982a, 171.

The date and author of the text is unknown. It seems to be incomplete. The extant two-hundred stanzas bear on signs of rainfall the prerequisite of agricultural production.

Viśvavallabha

Lang.: Sanskrit

Mss.: 1. Rajasthan Prachya Vidya Pratisthan, Jodhpur no. 5861–22 Lipisamaya [date of writing] saṁvat 1925, śaka 1790 (=1868/69). Complete in 540 ślokas. It is written in Devanāgarī characters in a style current in the nineteenth century. It is a copy made approximately two hundred and fifty years after the composition of the original. It contains many blank spaces which were perhaps lapses of the original one. Moreover there are several textual and metrical defects in it, too (Sadhale 2004, 102). 2. Vallabha Vaiṣṇava Maṭh, Nathdvār, Rajasthan, manuscript collection no. 195.7. The manuscript which belongs to Gosvāmījī Mahārāj Śrī Govind' lāljī the abbot of the temple (Das, 1988, 31) consists of 22 leaves. I was not able to see this manuscript.

Ed. transl.: Vishvavallabha ('Dear to the world': the science of plant life) transl. by Nalini Sadhale. Secunderabad 2004. (Agri-History Bulletin 5.) This edition and translation is based on the Jodhpur manuscript. – English translation of excerpts in AAI 24–33, 55–58. – Hindi translation by Shri Krishan 'Jugnu', Udaipur 2003.

Lit.: AAI 159. – Kaw 1971, 174. – Wojtilla 1982a, 167. – Das 1988, 31. – Abrol–Kanwar–Nene–Sadhale 2004.

The author of the work is Cakrapāṇi who lived and worked under the patronage of Mahārāṇa Pratāpsiṁha (1540–1597) of Mewar (Udaipur) of Rajasthan. According to B. M. Jawalia he was a brahmin of the Mathur subcaste and belonged to Nasavare Chobe family, enjoying the ancestrial title of 'Mishra' (Nene, Foreword). His work Viśvavallabha lit. 'Dear to the world' was likely composed in 1577 (Sadhale 2004, 96). The work is written mainly in verse form except some subtopics, which are in prose. Cakrapāṇi employed the following metres: anuṣṭubh, indravajrā, upajāti, upendravajrā, pṛthvī, mandākrāntā, mālinī, śārdūlavikrīḍita and sragdharā. He used a simple Sanskrit language which 'has, however, its own dignity and maturity'. The work contains nine chapters (ullāsa) divided into subchapters.

I. Groundwater: the lucky combinations in a dry region; the section on deserts; surface indications of groundwater on wetland; ordinary land/mountain land; indications of groundwater in mountains; rocks as surface indications of groundwater; soil as surface indication; vegetation as surface indication.

II. Water reservoirs: construction of water reservoirs.

III. Examination and suitability of ground: soil and propagation; trees near residence; plantation inside a fort.

IV. Propagation and plantation.

V. Water management.

VI. Protection and care.

VII. Nourishment and growth.

VIII. Diseases and treatments: wind related disorders; bile related disorders; phlegm related disorders; disease of indigestion caused by excessive watering; indigestion caused by excessive intake of food (manure); overmedication; insect related disorders; treatment of pruned trees; frost burn; fire burn; lightning; wind; friction; transplantation; trees ruined by animals; contact with unhealthy trees etc.; contrariety regarding seasons; lapses in the mode of treatment; discharge.

IX. Botanical wonders: wonders of seeds; wonders of trees; wonders with negative results; wonders of flowers; wonders of fruits (according to other experts – seedless fruits); naturally coloured cotton; improving quality of produce.

From this review on context it is easy to see that the work is neither kṛṣiśāstra nor vṛkṣāyurveda in the strict sense of terms. It is true that it closely resembles Sūrapāla's Vṛkṣāyurveda as far as it also deals with similar topics such as plant protection, treatment of the diseases of trees and botanical wonders (cf. Sadhale 2004, 95), however the chapters discussing groundwater, water reservoirs, examination of ground, water management etc. can be found in the Kāśyapīyakṛṣisūkti as well as the Hanumān mantra as we have already seen can be attested both in works on agriculture and horticulture proper. We can learn from Nene's scholarly study that the text has unique values concerning the detection of groundwater in arid, semi-arid, moist regions and hills in arid, the association of flora and fauna with groundwater and the like. The text throws light on various ways of agriculture and horticulture 'with a focus on the Mewar region of Rajasthan, which probably include adjacent areas of the present-day Gujarat and Madhya Pradesh' and as a whole 'offers us a wealth of prescriptions that could be researched further with the techniques available to us today' (Abrol–Kanwar–Nene–Sadhale 2004, 106–107 and 114).

Vyavasāyapraṣnottara or *Vyavasāyakramamu* or *Vyavasāyaśāstracarita*

Lang.: Telugu

Ed. transl.: No information. According to AAI 164 it seems to be a printed book which gives section on agriculture in questions and answers. To my best knowledge there is a book called Vyavasāyamu ('Agriculture') edited by Bhujaṅga Rāu Ellore, no date (Barnett 1912, 32). It is a modern work.

Saṁvatsaraphala

Lang.: Sanskrit

Mss.: Ms 34 398 Sarasvati Bhavan, Library (Tripathi 1971, 16) – as to the works attributed to various authors see CC I, 1122 and CC II, 681.

Ed. transl.: No information. Passages are given in Tripathi 1971 16, 17, 70, 74, 75, 88, 89, 90, 92, 95, 97, 164, 175 and 181.

Lit.: CC I, 1122 – CC II, 681. – Tirpathi 1971, 16.

These texts the date of which are unknown are almanacs containing information about the various products during the year. One of them is traditionally attributed to Varāhamihira, however it cannot be proved.

Sasyanandamu

Lang.: Telugu

Ed.: It has been published in Madras (personal communication Prof. Sankaranarayaran, director, S. V. U. Oriental Research Institute, Tirupati 28 November 1977); however, I have failed to procure any copy so far.

Lit.: Sivanārayya 1980, 485 – Wojtilla 1982, 170.

The author of the text Donayāmātya lived in the 14th century (Sivanārayya 1980, 485). It is a textbook (śāstragrantam) on agriculture and related topics.

Sasyanandamu

Lang.: Telugu

Ed.: No information.

Lit.: AAI Wojtilla 1982, 170.

According to Prof. S. Sankaranarayaran, director, S. V. U. Oriental Research Institute (personal communication, Tirupati 28 November 1977) the text was composed by Addaṅki Liṅga Kavi who lived in the 12th century. I was unable to verify this statement so far on the ground of the textbooks and encyclopedia studied in India and elsewhere.

Sasyanandamu

Lang.: Telugu

Ed.: Sasyanandamu by Lakṣmīnṛsimha Śāstri, Masulipatam 1931. This very rare book printed only in 125 copies one of which is kept at the India Office Library (= British Library) under the signature Telugu D. 1987.

We could not find any reference to this text in the secondary literature. It looks like a poem. According to the title page the author Lakṣmīnṛsiṁha Śāstri was the son of Calla Nāgaliṅga Śāstri, resident of Maculipatnam (Masulipatam). From the preface we learn that the author has heavily drawn upon Varāhamihira' Bṛhatsaṁhitā (Nene).

Sasyānanda

Lang.: Sanskrit

Ed.: No information

Ms.: One manuscript from the private collection of the ruler of Vijayanagar (Oppert 1880, No. 7445) and two copies possessed by a certain Taḍakamalla Veṅkatakṛṣṇayārar from Tiruvallīkeṇī (Oppert 1885, No. 3289) have been reported. The author of this work is unknown (Law 1918, 259). There is an another text under the same title authored by a certain Kaideva which has some bearing on agriculture and botany and quoted three times in the Nirṇaya-sindhu (Law 1918, 262).

Lit.: Oppert 1880 and 1885 – Law 1918, 259 and 262 – AAI 164. – Wojtilla 1982, 170.

The text entitled 'Pleasure of crops' looks like a poem but nothing definite can be said before a scrutiny of the manuscripts is completed. Unfortunately, the editor of the catalogue, Oppert, knew a great deal of manuscripts only from hearsay (cf. CC I, VII.). It is not clear whether this Sanskrit work has anything to do with the Telugu texts called Sasyanandamu. I was told by the editors of NCC in the Department of Sanskrit at Madras University on 19th November 1977 that there was no hope to find out these manuscripts.

APPENDIX ONE

Texts containing independent chapter(s) on kr̥ṣi

Agnipurāṇa

Lang.: Sanskrit

Ed.: Agnipurāṇa ed. by Ācārya Baladeva Upādhyāya Varanasi 1966 (Kashi Sanskrit Series 174)

Transl.: – by N. Gangadharan. Vols. I.–IV. Delhi–Varanasi–Patna 1987.

Lit.: Rocher 1986, 134–137 – Gopal 1973, 158–159.

This is a typical encyclopedic work which contains in chapter 121 highly important information on agriculture which can be aptly compared with the respective portions of the Kr̥ṣiparāśara. Among others the text lists six basic agricultural operations: goṣṭhayātrā 'festival of the cow-pen', kr̥ṣikarmasamācaraṇa 'the usual method of agricultural work', bījavāpana 'sowing seeds', dhānyaccheda 'harvesting of paddy', dhānyapraveśa 'bringing in paddy' i. e. 'storing paddy' and dhānyaniṣkramaṇa 'taking out paddy'. The third and fourth have the same name in the Kr̥ṣiparāśara, other two have slightly different names that while the sixth one is missing there. It shows that perhaps 'both the texts refer roughly to the same period', however the similarities in expression and contents do not allow us to think of a common source of them. Although the Agnipurāṇa also contains a Hanumān mantra its wording differs from the respective mantra in the Kr̥ṣiparāśara and so its aim is also different (Gopal 1973, 158–159).

Ajitāgama

Lang.: Sanskrit

Ed.: Ajitāgama, édition critique. I–II. par N. R. Bhatt. Pondichéry 1963–1967. (Publications de L' Institut Français d' Indologie 24.)

Transl.: No information.

It is a Śaiva handbook on temple-building, image-making and religious practice. Farquhar conjecturally places in the seventh-eighth centuries A. D. (Farquhar 1920, 194). The paṭala seventh is devoted to the work of ploughing in ritual context.

Amarakośa

Lang.: Sanskrit

Ed.: – critically edited with English equivalents for each word by N. G. Sardesai and D. G. Padhye. Poona 1969^{2}.

Lit.: Maity 1970, 102–103, 108–110. – Wojtilla 1989, 102.

Being the most celebrated Sanskrit lexicon composed by Amarasiṁha around the sixth century A. D. It contains in book two chapter 9 verses 6–77 a very rich vocabulary of agriculture comprising a highly valuable description of agricultural implements, operations and products (Maity 1970, 102–103 and 108–110 respectively). Especially important are its data on husking of corn is identical with the modern practice (Maity 1970, 103) and that of the so-called ard-plough consisting of four main parts (Wojtilla 1989, 102).

Atrisaṁhitā or - *Samūrtārcanādhikaraṇa* 'Treatise on the image cult' Gonda 1977, 144)

Ed.: – by V. Raghunāthacakravarti Bhaṭṭācārya and M. Rāmakṛṣṇakavi. Tirupati 1943 (Śrīveṅkateśvara Oriental Series 6.).

Transl.: According to Gonda the text was being translated by C. van der Burg (Utrecht) (Gonda 1977, 144, note 35). There is no further information about this undertaking.

It is a ritual handbook of the Vaikhānasas and an elaborate and valuable treatment of the image cult (Gonda 1977, 144). The adhyāya three, lines 6–8 give useful advices on the plough.

Arthaśāstra

Ed.: The Kauṭilīya Arthaśāstra Part I. A critical edition with a glossary by R. P. Kangle. Bombay 1969. – Kauṭilīyamarthaśāstram with four commentaries. Ed. by V. S. Dātāra. Varanasi 1991 (adhikaraṇas 1–7).

Transl.: Kauṭilya's Arthaśāstra transl. by R. Shamasastry. Bangalore 1915. – Das altindische Buch vom Welt- und Staatsleben. Das Arthaçāstra des Kauṭilya übers. von J. J. Meyer- Leipzig 1926. – Arthashastra ili nauka politiki perevod s sanskrita izdanie podgotovil V. I. Kal'yanov. Moskva–Leningrad 1959. – An English translation by R. P. Kangle. Bombay 1972[2].

Lit.: Laping 1982, 103–110, 154. Wojtilla 1997–1998 – Hota 1999 – Nene 2002 – Sinha 2003 – Wojtilla forthcoming.

The chapter 42 (section 41) called 'The superintendent of crown-lands (in the country)' (Sītādhyakṣarakaraṇa) is the so far earliest longer and comprehensive discussion of some important aspects of agriculture. Laping is right saying that this chapter gives only allusions to the actual practice (Laping 1982, 154). In my view it is a collection of statements based on theory as well as on practical observations. It has not any touch of proper editorial work so it is not a coherent treatment of the subject. The main points are as follows. It clearly distinguishes the science of agriculture and the science of horticulture; there is a detailed description of the most important agricultural operations such as ploughing, sowing, irrigation, storing grain an also of different people involved in these works. For textual and semantical problems we are far from a quite satisfactory understanding of all issues raised in the chapter (cf. Wojtilla 1997–1998 and forthcoming).

Kalittokai

Lang.: Tamil

Lit.: Zvelebil 1975, 100–101.

'The anthology in the kali metre' contains 150 poems. The third section i. e. poems 66–100 deal with marutam ('agricultural') situations (Zvelebil 1975, 100). The text is dated from the fourth-sixth century (Zvelebil 1975, 101).

Kāśyapajñānakāṇḍa

Ed.: – ed. by Pārthasārathi Bhaṭṭācārya. Tirupati 1948. (second edition 1960).

Transl.: Kāśyapa's book of wisdom transl. by T. Goudriaan. The Hague 1965. (Disputationes Rhenotrajectinae 10.)

It is a text of the Vaikhānasas from the second half of the first millennium A. D. (Goudriaan 1965, 9). The chapters 22 and 92 provide us with important information about the plough and ploughing in a ritual context.

Kāśyapaśilpa

Ed. and transl.: Kāśyapaśilpam [ed. by] V. G. Apte. Poona 1926. (Ānandāśramasaṁskṛtagranthāvali 5.) – (With Marathi transl.) by R. P. Kulkarni. Mumbaī 1987.

Lit.: Winternitz 1967, 614.

It is a text on architecture which describes also the form of images of different gods. The age of the work is unknown. According to the editor it was probably written after the reign of the Nanda-kings, but this is only a conjecture (Winternitz 1967, 614). KāŚilpa I, 54–53 gives a unique account of the plough abounding in peculiar terms denoting parts of the plough.

Tiruvaḷḷuvar

Lang.: Tamil

Ed. transl.: G. U. Pope: The 'Sacred' Kurraḷ of Tiruvaḷḷuva Nâyanâr. London 1886.

Lit.: V. V. S. Aiyar: Agricultural maxims of the poet Tiruvalluvar. in: Agri – History 2 (1998), 59–61.

This most famous work of Tamil literature composed by Vaḻḻuvar and most probably dated from the fifth-sixth century A. D. is a collection of 1330 epigrams which contains some stanzas on agriculture in chapter two concerning artha i. e. politics.

Devala

Lang.: Sanskrit

Ed.: See Jyotistattva. – Vācaspatyam III, 2209. – Majumdar–Banerji 1960 passim.

Transl.: No information.

Lit.: Majumdar–Banerji 1960 passim – Winternitz 1967, 654. – Tripathi 1971, 6.

Devala the astronomer is a predecessor of Varāhamihira (Winternitz 1967, 654). His work has not come down to us, however he has been frequently quoted by Varāhamihira and his commentator Bhaṭṭotpala who flourished in the tenth century. In this manner Tripathi dates Devala from a period prior to the ninth century (Tripathi 1971, 6). The verses attributed to him by Raghunandana are the following number of the Kṛṣiparāśara: 130b, 131, 133b, 135a, 143, 144, 145b, 147a, 148a, 177, 178b and 179a. Curiously these verses bear on ploughing and sowing and not on climatology.

Nālaṭiyār 'The great quatrains'or Nālaṭinā̱nuru 'The four hundred quatrains'

Ed.: There are numerous editions of the text.

Lang.: Tamil

Transl.: The Naladiyar or four hundred quatrains in Tamil by G. U. Pope. Oxford 1893.

Lit.: AAI 164. – Zvelebil 1975, 122–123.

This is an anthology, a part of it belongs to the heading poṟul 'wealth' (Zvelebil 1975, 122–123) and gives some reference to agriculture (AAI 164).

Parāśarasmṛti

Lang.: Sanskrit

Ed.: with Mādhava's commentary by V. S. Islampulkar. Bombay 1893–1911.

Transl.: The institutes of Parāśara translated into English by K. K. Bhattacharya. Calcutta 1887 (BI N. S. 567.)

Lit.: Banerji 1971, 78 and 116.

The date is unknown. It is earlier than the Yājñavalkyasmṛti (Banerji 1971, 78). which can be placed in the first centuries of the Christian era or earlier (Banerji 1971, 116). Chapter two propounds the law relating to the duties prescribed for a householder in the Kali age with special emphasis on agriculture.

Perumpāṇāṟṟuppaṭai

Lang.: Tamil

Ed. transl.: Pattupattu. Ten Tamil idylls. Translated into English verse by J. V. Chelliah. Madras 1862.

Lit.: Zvelebil 1975, 46.

It may be dated roughly between 100 B. C. and A. D. 200 (Zvelebil 1975, 46). The poet draws a fine picture of the country around the capital Kanchipuram. The lines 180–300 provide us with a vivid description of village life including the basic agricultural operations.

Bṛhatparāśarasmṛti or *Bṛhatparāśarasaṁhitā*

Lang.: Sanskrit

Ed.: Dharmaśāstrasaṁgraha ed. by Jībananda Vidyāsāgara. Calcutta, 1876, II, 54–309: this text is very corrupt at places. – Vācaspatyam III 2201 – 2205: it gives some plausible and some highly conjectural emendations.

Transl.: No information.

Lit.: Gopal 1963/64 27. – Kane 1968, 466. – Wojtilla 1986. – Wojtilla 1993, 528.

The dating of the text can be based on considerations of comparative law history and so it remains absurdly vague. According to Kane it appears to be a late work, it is a recast of the Parāśarasmṛti (Kane 1968, 466). Derrett tentatively dates it from the period between A. D. 1100–1400 (Derrett–Wojtilla 1986, 361). The chapter three on the duties and manners of a householder, agriculture, honour to cows contains a valuable description of the plough (in Jībananda Vidyāsāgara's edition pp. 101–117 cf. Gopal 1963/64, 27). This portion of the chapter has been translated into English by Wojtilla (Wojtilla 1986, 363–364). This description has likely been adopted by Daśarathaśāstrī the author of Kṛṣiśāsana (Wojtilla 1993, 528).

Bṛhatsaṁhitā

Lang.: Sanskrit

Ed. transl.: Varāhamihira's Bṛhat Saṁhitā with English translation by R. Bhat. Delhi–Varanasi–Patna–Madras 1981.

Lit.: Maity 1970, 106–107, 245.

Chapter fourty called 'Growth of crops' (Sasyajātaka) forms a minor treatise on agricultural climatology. Beside that the following passages bear on agriculture and related subjects: III, 5, 16, 29; IV, 16; V, 5, 20, 22, 23, 79, 85, 96; V, 21, 24, 27, 34, 38, 39, 52, 54, 61, 75, 76, 78, 90, 92; VII, 4, 10, 11, 14, 16, 19, 40; VIII, 8, 9, 12, 13, 30, 36, 47, 50; IX, 14, 20, 26, 35, 40, 42, 43; X, 5–6, 11, 13, 18; XIII, 8; XVII, 14, 15, 17, 18–19; XVIII, 2, 3; XIX, 1, 4–6, 7–9, 10–12, 13–14, 16–18, 19–21; XXII, 5; XXIV, 23, 24, 33, 36; XXV, 2, 5; XXVII, 1, 6, 8; XXIX, 2, 3, 4, 5; XXXI, 1; XXXII, 10; XXXIV, 12; XXXV, 5; XXXIX, 4 XLV, 4–6; XLVI, 42; XLVII, 16 (cf. Maity 1970, 245). Being probably composed in the sixth century the text is very important for the study of the history of kṛṣiśāstra. A striking feature of the text is that it has reference to summer crops (IX, 43), autumnal crops (V, 27) and vernal crops (XXVII, 1) (cf. Maity 1970, 106).

Brahmapurāṇa

Lang.: Sanskrit

Ed.: Gṛhastharatnākara. A treatise on Smṛti by Candeṣvara Ṭhakkura ed. by Mahāmahopadhyāya Kamalakṛṣṇa Smṛtitīrtha. Calcutta 1928 (Bibliotheca Indica 249), 432–433.

Lit.: Rocher 1986, 155.

As a matter of fact the extant Brahmapurāṇa itself is also regarded merely as a conglomerate of passages from different periods and hands (Rocher 1986, 155).

This excerpt embeded in the duties of the householder gives advices on rituals of the commencement of agriculture, ploughing, sowing and the proper care of cows and bulls. This portion of the text cannot be attested in the extant editions of the Brahmapurāṇa.

Mānasāra

Lang.: Sanskrit

Ed.: Architecture and sculpture. Sanskrit text with critical notes by P. K. Acharya, Manasara Series III, London 1934.

Transl.: Manasara [sic!] translated from original Sanskrit by P. K. Acharya. Manasara Series IV, London 1934.

The text deals with building of temples and houses, planning of cities and villages, installation of idols etc. in 58 chapters. The chapter five called bhūparīkṣāvidhānam ('The examination of soil') gives an excellent description of the plough and its accesories. According to Acharya it is a work of the sixth or seventh century A. D. (cf. Winternitz 1967, 609) while Banerji places it in the period between the eleventh-fifteenth centuries A. D. (Banerji 1971, 243).

Raṭṭamata or *Raṭṭasūtra*

Ed.: – by H. Sesha Iyengar. Madras 1950.

Ms.: One palm-leaf manuscript belongs to the Mackenzie collection (Wilson 1828[2], 303).

It was translated by Bhāskara, son of Nagaya into Telugu and dedicated to Venkatapati Palliyar of Eravar in the 14th century (Law 1918, 277; cf. Bandhyopadhyaya 1925, I, 15). To my best knowledge the Telugu version is still unedited.

Lit.: Wilson 1828, 303 – Law 1918, 277 – Bandhyopadhyaya 1925, I, 15 – AAI 164. – Wojtilla 1982a, 170.

According to the AAI (170) this Kanarese text deals with forecast of rain and other agricultural matters. The Telugu text contains astrological predictions of the weather, rain, drought and similar topics applicable to agriculture and the plenty or scarcity of grain. The author of the text is Ratta or Retta. (Wilson 1828[2], 303 cf. Law 1918, 277).

Lokopakāra

Ed.: Lokopakāra of Cāvuṇḍarāja. Madras 1950.

Transl.: No information.

Lit.: AAI 164. – Wojtilla 1982a, 170.

This Kanarese text contains a section on science of agriculture and plant life (AAI 170).

Vaikhānāsāgama or *Marīcīsaṁhitā* or *Vimānārcanākalpa* 'Procedure of the image cult'

(Gonda 1977, 144, note 38).

Ed.: Marīcīsaṁhitā ed. by D. Raṅgācārya. Īgāvāripālem 1927 (in Telugu characters, it is the best edition) – The Vaikhānasāgama of Marīci. Ed. by Sāmbaśiva Śāstrī. Trivandrum 1935. (Trivandrum Sanskrit Series 121.) It is of poor philological value. – Extracts in: Colas 1986, 213–254.

Transl.: Extracts in French translation in: Colas 1986, 89–212.

Lit.: Colas 1986.

It is a Vaikhānasa work which includes among its prescriptions pertaining to temple-cult, extensive expositions about the building of temples. It was perhaps composed before the eighth century A. D. (Colas 1986, 7). The paṭala three is description of the plough and the ploughing in ritual context.

Vaijayantīkośa

Ed.: – of Ṣrī Yādavaprakāśācārya. Ed. by Haragovinda Śāstrī. Varanasi 1971.

It is a voluminous lexicon dating back to about the middle of the eleventh century. Chapter III, 8 verses 17–67 are bearing on agriculture.

Vyavahārapradīpikā

Ed. transl.: No information.

Mss.: There is an extant manuscript in Maithili characters in the Darbhanga Rāj Library, Darbhanga (AAI 161).

The author of the text is a certain Hudrahastaka Harapati Ṭhākur who lived around 1500 A. D. A section goes on sowing and acts to be performed by agriculturists. AAI inaccurately gives the title as Vivahara Pradipika (AAI 161).

Śivāyana or *Śibāyan*

Ed.: Śivāyana – with a life of the author by Īśāna Chandra Vasu. Calcutta 1903[2]. – Śivāyan by Rāmeśvar. Calcutta 1957.

Transl.: No information.

Lit.: Das Gupta 1935, 265–266. – Chaudhuri 1939, 183. – Novikova 1965, 119. – Zbavitel 1976, 189. – Sen 1979[3], 151.

Written probably in in 1711 this book describes the domestic life of Śiva, a poor farmer who had to strive hard for livelihood (Zbavitel 1976, 189 cf. Novikova 1965, 119). As a cultivator he ploughs his fields, sows seeds, takes out weeds, cuts grass and binding it into a sheef, carries those on his head (Chaudhuri 1939, 183). The poem bears good evidence of a very low level of agrarian economy in South-west Bengal which had always been a purely rice-producing area (Sen 1979[3], 151). The work gives a true picture of agricultural operations and among others narrates how Śiva and his assistant weed out the tares with great zeal and planted their seedlings of paddy and raised ridges in the field (Das Gupta 1935, 266).

APPENDIX TWO

Collections of agricultural sayings in vernaculars others than ascribed to authors

Research into popular sayings is an old debt of Indian studies. It must be carried out on regional level. Here I list only a handful data gained from handbooks and bibliographies.

Bengali: Vandhyopadhyay 1893. – Chakravarti 1930. – S. K. De (ed.): Bāṁlā prabād chḁṛā o calti kathā ('Bengali proverbs, rhymes and colloquial sayings'). Calcutta 1952^2: it contains numerous sayings bearing on agriculture and related subjects.

Bihari: Behar proverbs: Christian 1986, 200–223: Class V. Proverbs relating to agriculture and seasons.

Hindi: S. P. Tivari: Khetī kī kahāvateṅ. 1949.

Kanarese: In: BDAGM No 35. (1934)

Malayalam: Kr̥ṣipāṭṭu is the collective name of folk songs relating to agriculture. There are several types of songs sung by the peasants during the various operations. Peasants describe their traditional method of cultivation in their songs (Choondal 1980, 24–25). Some songs praise the cultivation of paddy and coconuts, many of them have no idea to convey, but have lift and rhytm which inspire the workers engaged in hard manual work (George 1968, 22). A collection of them was published in BDAGM No. 36 (1935). The title Krsi-patta given in AAI 165 is incorrect.

Oriya: Majumdar – Banerji 1960 in the bibliography at the end of their edition mention a collection of agricultural sayings in Orissa which they could consult through the courtesy of Dr Parija, Cuttack.

Rajasthani: Rājasthānī Krishikalā Vateṁ [sic!] Ed. by J. S. Gahlot. (cf. Sircar 1965, 26.) – Farmers IV, 106–107 (Rajasthani-English).

Sanskrit: Proverbs bearing on kr̥ṣi in: L. Sternbach: Mahā-subhāṣita-saṁgraha VI. ed. by S. Bhaskaran Nair. Hoshiarpur 1987. nos. 11235–11241 H.

Tamil: In: BDAGM No. 29 (1928) – E. L. Kandasami.: Velanmai pazhamozhigal (Agricultural proverbs). Coimbatore 1983[4].

Telugu: A collection of Telugu sayings and proverbs bearing on agriculture [With preface by C. Benson]. in: BDAGM 22 (1891), 175–209. M. Suguna sri collected and analysed 500 proverbs bearing on agriculture (Suguna sri 2004).

A special branch of living tradition represented by the almanacs (jantrī or pañcāṅga). There is an unpublished Ph.D. thesis on the subject: S. K. Mishra: Weather forecasting in almanacs relating to farming operations and its relevance in today's agriculture. Institute of Agricultural Sciences, Banaras Hindu University, Varanasi 1998, 257 pp. I have not consulted it yet.

Note: This collection of bibliographical data is of course preliminary since no one has a complete overview of folkloristic research in India.

APPENDIX THREE

Texts on tanks and wells

There are numerous works on tanks (taḍāga) and wells (kūpa) and they still await for publication. Strictly speaking these texts are not works proper on agriculture but one must keep in mind that real kṛṣiśāstras such as the Kāśyapīyakṛṣisūkti, works of mixed character such as the Viśvavallabha and works on horticulture such as the the Vṛkṣāyurveda of Sūrapāla pay special attention to digging wells and to tanks and consequently contain a separate chapter bearing on the subject. Chapter 35 of Matsyapurāṇa deals with the establishment of tanks, pleasure gardens and wells and the like. On the other hand I would not list chapter fifty-four of the Bṛhatsaṁhitā of Varāhamihira in the group of such texts although the latter deals with exploration of water springs (dakārgala) an essential part of well-digging etc. Similarly the establishment of wells or tanks in the courtyards of houses or pleasure-gardens of palaces are also out of scope of our subject. Since we could not see the manuscripts of the single items we follow the reliable catalogues which have not allow me in every case to make clear distinction between technical texts (jyotiṣa or śilpa) and dharmaśāstras in the widest sense of the term: quite frequently these texts speak of consecration, dedication or donation of tanks and wells. It woud be beyond the scope of our present work to give a list of these texts: as to works on kūpas cf. NCC IV, 262–263 and concerning taṭākas/taḍāgas cf. NCC VIII, 14. A special attention deserves the text called taḍāgādividhi which is kept at the Library of the Asiatic Society of Bengal Calcutta under the signature Ms 3406 (AAI 162).

APPENDIX FOUR

Works recorded in AAI waiting for verification

Muni Bhovabodhini by Narayana-Gajapati Bentalori – 'A Sanskrit work in Telugu script with Telugu translation' (AAI 154) = Munibhavabodini by Narain Dantalori – 'A Sanskrit work dealing with agriculture in one of the sections in Telugu script, with translation in Telugu' (AAI 165).

Bibliography and abbreviations

AAH Asian Agri-History, Secunderabad, A. P. India.

AAI Agriculture in ancient India. Ed. by D. Raghavan, New Delhi 1964.

ABORI Annals of the Bhandarkar Oriental Research Institute, Poona.

Abrol 2004 I. P. Abrol's review on Sadhale Nalini (Tr.) Vishvavallabha. in: AAH 8:3 (2004), 241–244.

AL A preliminary report of the Saṁskr̥t and Prakrit manuscripts in the Adyar Library. Madras 1910.

AOF Altorientalische Forschungen

AOH Acta Orientalia Academiae Scientiarum Hungaricae

AmaK Amarakośa

ArthŚā Arthaśāstra of Kauṭilya.

AT Antik Tanulmányok (Classical Studies) Budapest

Aufrecht 1869 Th. Aufrecht: A catalogue of Sanskrit manuscripts of the Library of Trinity College Cambridge. Cambridge–London 1869.

Ayangarya 2003 V. S. Ayangarya: Some comments on Krishi-Parashara. in: AAH 7:1 (2003), 55–58.

Ayangarya 2004 V. S. Ayangarya: Krishi-Parashara: rainfall prediction and adhika masa. in: AAH 8:1 (2004), 63–66.

Bandhyopadhyaya 1925 N. C. Bandhopadhyaya: Economic life and progress in ancient India. vol. I. Calcutta 1925.

Banerji 1955 S. C. Banerji: Kr̥ṣi-Parāśara a work on agriculture. In: ABORI XXXVI. (1955), 1–26.

Banerji 1971 S. C. Banerji: A companion to Sanskrit literature. Delhi–Varanasi–Patna, 1971.

Barnett 1912 L. D. Barnett: A catalogue of the Telugu books in the Library of the British Museum. London 1912.

Barua 1933 K. L. Barua: Early history of Kāmarūpa. Shillong 1933.

Basak 1969 Rāmacaritam of Sandhyākaranandin. Ed. by Haraprasād Śāstri. Revised with English translation and notes by R. Basak. Calcutta 1969.

BDAGM Bulletin of the Department of Agriculture, Government of Madras.

Bedekar 1992 V. V. Bedekar: Agriculture in ancient India. Papers presented at the seminar conducted on Saturday, 25th April, 1992 at Thane, under the auspices of the Institute for Oriental Study, Thane. [Thane 1992]

Benthley 1800 J. Benthley: A historical view of the Hindu astronomy from the earliest dawn of that science in India to the present time. in: Asiatic Researches VI. Calcutta 1800.

BGOML Bulletin of the Government Oriental Manuscript Library, Madras.

Bhatt 1997 S. C. Bhatt (ed.): The encyclopaedic district gazetteers of India. Southern zone (vol. 2.) New Delhi 1997.

Bhattacharyya 1976 S. K. Bhattacharyya: Farmers, rituals and modernization. A sociological study. Calcutta 1976.

BI N. S. Bibliotheca Indica, New Series

Birwe 1964 R. Birwe's review on Majumdar–Banerji 1960. in: ZDMG 114 (1964), 455–457.

BMM Bulletin of the Madras Museum

BMPP British Museum Printed Books

BṛKaŚlSaṁ Bṛhatkathāślokasaṁgraha a study by V. S. Agrawala. With Sanskrit text edited by P. K. Agrawala. Varanasi 1974.

Brown 1980 C. P. Brown: Dictionary Telugu–English. New Delhi 1980[2].

B. S. Bengali Saṁvat

Cakradhara Cakradhara's Nyāyamañjarī-Granthibhaṅga quoted after Das 1988.

Caland 1929 see VaikhāSmS

Carnegie 1853 Carnegie: Kutcherry technicalities. Allahabad 1853.

CC Catalogus catalogorum I.–III. Leipzig 1891–1903.

CCBM Catalogus catalogorum of Bengali manuscripts. Vol. I. Compiled and edited by J. M. Bhattacharjee. Calcutta 1978.

CCDPL A comprehensive and critical dictionary of the Prakrit languages. With special reference to Jain literature. Vol. I. Fasc. I. General editor A. M. Ghatage. Poona 1993.

Chakravarti 1930 Meteorological proverbs of Bengal. Edited and translated by Ch. Chakravarti. in: JPROASB (NS) 26 (1930), 371–377.

Chatterji 1926 S. K. Chatterji: The origin and development of the Bengali language. Calcutta 1926.

Chatterji 1960[2] S. K. Chatterji: Indo-Aryan and Hindi. Calcutta 1960[2].

Chaudhuri 1935 N. N. Chaudhuri: Ḍākārṇava. Calcutta 1935.

Chaudhuri 1939 Nanimadhab Chaudhuri: Rudra – Śiva – as an agricultural deity. in: IHQ XV (1939), 183–196.

Choondal 1980 Chummar Choondal: Kerala folk literature. Trichur 1980.

Choudhary 1971 A. K. Choudhary: Early medieval village in North-Eastern India. A. D. 600–1200. Calcutta 1971.

Choudhury 1959 P. C. Choudhury: The history of civilisation of the people of Assam to the twelfth century A. D. Gauhati 1959.

Chowdhury 1992 K. A. Chowdhury: Kṛṣi – Parāśara. in: IJHS 27(1) (1992), 31–50.

Christian 1986 J. Christian: Behar proverbs. Classified and arranged by –. New Delhi 1986. (first edition 1891)

Colas 1986 G. Colas: Le temple selon Marīci. Extraits de la Marīcisaṁhitā étudiés, édités et traduits. Pondichéry 1986. (Publications de l' Institut Français d' Indologie 71.)

CPMOIL Catalogue of Persian manuscripts in the Library of the India Office by H. Ethe. Vol. I. Oxford 1903.

Das 1988 R. P. Das: Das Wissen von der Lebensspanne der Bäume. Sūrapāla's Vṛkṣāyurveda kritisch ediert, übersetzt und kommentiert von –. Stuttgart 1988.

Das 1997 R. P. Das: On the Vṛkṣāyurveda of Parāśara [A review of: Vṛkṣāyurveda of Parāśara (A treatise on plant science). edited by N. N. Sircar and Roma Sarkar. Delhi 1996)]. in: JEĀS 5 (1997), 197–215.

Das Gupta 1935 T. C. Das Gupta: Aspects of Bengali society from old Bengali literature. Calcutta 1935.

Derrett Personal communication by Prof. J. M. Duncan Derrett.

Datta 1987 A. Datta (ed.): Encyclopaedia of Indian literature. Vol. I. New Delhi 1987.

Datta 1988 A. Datta (ed.) Encyclopaedia of Indian literature. Vol. II. New Delhi 1988.

De 1960 S. K. De's Foreword to Majumdar–Banerji 1960, see Kṛṣiparāśara editions.

Deussen 1920 P. Deussen: Allgemeine Geschichte der Philosophie. I, 1. Vierte Auflage. Leipzig 1920.

Drav. Enc. Dravidian Encyclopaedia vol. II. Thiruvanthapuram 1993.

Edgerton 1931 F. Edgerton (transl.) The elephant-sport (Matanga-Lila) of Nilakantha. New Haven 1931.

Farmers IV Farmers of India vol. IV. Madhya Pradesh, Rajasthan, Gujarat, Maharashtra by M. S. Randhawa, V. Nath, Suresh Vaidya,, H. M. Patel, M. D. Patel and B. S. Kadam. New Delhi 1968.

Farquhar 1920 J. N. Farquhar: An outline of the religious literature of India. Oxford 1920.

Gangopadhyaya 1932 R. Gangopadhyaya: Some materials for the study of agriculture and agriculturists in ancient India. Serampore 1932.

Gangopadhyaya 1941 R. Gangopadhyaya: Agriculture in ancient India. in: Dacca University Studies 1941, 101–126.

Ganguly 1930–1931 R. Ganguly (= Gangopadhyaya): Cultivation in ancient India. Introduction. in: IHQ 6 (1930), 737–746 and Cultivation in ancient India II. in: IHQ 7 (1931), 19–27.

Gazetteer III The Imperial Gazetteer of India. New Edition Oxford 1907–1909. vol. III.

George 1968 K. M. George: A survey of Malayalam literature. London 1968.

Ghosa 1908 Devanārāyaṇa Ghosa: Brahmaputra – upadhyāy prāchina kavi. Calcutta 1908.

Gode 1943 P. K. Gode: Some notes on the history of Indian dietetics with special reference to the history of jalebī. in: NIA 6: 8–9. November-December 1943, 169–181.

Gode 1948 P. K. Gode's paper in: Poona Orientalist 13 (1948) was not available to me. I quote it on the ground of Kaw 1971.

Gombrich 1988 R. F. Gombrich: Theravāda Buddhism. A social history from ancient Benares to modern Colombo. London–New York 1988.

Gonda 1954 J. Gonda: Aspects of early Viṣṇuism. Utrecht 1954.

Gonda 1977 J. Gonda: Medieval religious literature in Sanskrit. Wiesbaden 1977. (A history of Indian Literature II.1.)

Gopal 1963/64 Lallanji Gopal: Technique of agriculture in early medieval India. in: University of Allahabad Historical Studies, Ancient India Section. Allahabad 1963/64, 1–37.

Gopal 1973 Lallanji Gopal: The date of the Kṛṣi – Parāśara. in: JIH 1973, 152–168.

Gopal 1980 Lallanji Gopal: Aspects of history of agriculture in ancient India. Varanasi 1980

Gopal 1981 The Gurusaṁhitā. An ancient text on weather-forecasting. Editor Lallanji Gopal. Varanasi 1981. Monographs of the Department of Ancient Indian History, Culture & Archaeology. No. 10.

Gopal 1983 Lallanji Gopal: The date of the Gurusaṁhitā. in: Rangavalli. Recent researches in Indology. Sri S. R. Rao Felicitation Volume. Editors A. V. Narasimha Murthi, B. K. Gururaja Rao. Delhi 1983, 317–329.

Gopal 1984 Lallanji Gopal: Cultural material in the Gurusaṁhitā. in: Religion and Society in ancient India. Sudhakar Chattopadhyaya Commemoration volume. Ed. by Pranabananda Jash. Calcutta 1984, 361–370.

Goudriaan 1965 Kāśyapajñānakāṇḍa. Kāśyapa's book of wisdom. A ritual handbook of the Vaikhānasas. Translated and annotated by –. The Hague 1965.

Grierson 1885 G. A. Grierson: Bihar peasant life. Calcutta 1885.

Hota 1999 K. N. Hota: Function of Sītādhyakṣa. in: Kauṭilya's Arthaśāstra and social welfare. Ed. by V. N. Jha, Delhi 1999, 77–82.

IHQ Indian Historical Quarterly

IIJ Indo-Iranian Journal

IJHS Indian Journal of History of Science

Indike Arrian with an English translation by P. A. Brunt. Cambridge Mass. 1983.

IOL India Office Library (= British Library)

JA Journal Asiatique

JAOS Journal of the American Oriental Society

JASB Journal of the Asiatic Society of Bengal

JEĀS Journal of the European Āyurvedic Society

Jesudasan 1961 C. Jesudasan–H. Jesudasan: A history of Tamil literature. Calcutta 1961.

JPROASB Journal and Proceedings of the Asiatic Society of Bengal.

JAS (L) Journal of the Asiatic Society, Letters

KalāVi Kalāvilāsa of Kṣemendra. in: Minor works of Kṣemendra. Ed. by E. V. V. Rāghavāchārya and D. G. Padhye. Hyderabad 1961, 219–271.

Kane 1968 P. V. Kane: History of Dharmaśāstra I. 1. Revised and enlarged. Poona 1968.

Kanwar 2004 J. S. Kanwar: Some comments on Vishvavallabha. in: AAH 8:3 (2004), 239–240.

Kaw 1971 R. K. Kaw: Peeps into agriculture in ancient India. In: VIJ 9(1971), 164–168.

KāmaSū Mallanāga Vātsyāyana: Kāmasūtra edited by D. Sastri. Benares 1964.

Kosambi 1970 D. D. Kosambi: The culture and civilisation of ancient India in historical outline. New Delhi 1970.

KṛtyaKaT DānaK Kṛtyakalpataru Dānakāṇḍa quoted after Gopal 1973, 167.

Kuiper 1969 Kuiper's review on Majumdar–Banerji 1960. in: IIJ 11 (1968–69) 213–216.

Lal 1980 Acche Lāl: Prācīn Bhārat meṅ kr̥ṣi. Vārāṇasī 1980.

Laping 1979 J. Laping: Ancient technology of irrigation in India. in: Asie du Sud. Traditions et changements. Paris (1979) 43–49.

Laping 1982 J. Laping: Die landwirtschaftliche Produktion in Indien. Ackerbau-Technologie und traditionale Agrargesellschaft dargestellt nach dem Arthaśāstra und Dharmaśāstra. Wiesbaden 1982 (Beiträge zur Südasien-Forschung Südasien-Institut Universität Heidelberg 62).

Law 1918 N. N. Law: Vârttâ. in: IA XLII (1918), 233–241, 256–253, and 275–279.

LiṅgaP Liṅgapurāṇa, Bombay 1924, Veṅkateśvara Press.

MahāBh Vyākaraṇamahābhāṣya of Patañjali. Ed. by F. Kielhorn. Bombay 1885–1906. (Bombay Sanskrit and Prakrit Series)

MahāBhā The Mahābhārata. Text as constituted in its critical edition. Vols. I.–V. Poona 1971–1976.

Maity 1970 S. K. Maity: Economic life in northern India in the Gupta period. Delhi–Patna–Varanasi 1970^2

Majumdar 1927 G. P. Majumdar: Vanaspati. Plants and plant-life as in Indian treatises and tradition. Calcutta 1927.

Majumdar 1935 G. P. Majumdar: Upavana-vinoda (A Sanskrit treatise on arbori-horticulture). Calcutta 1935. (Indian Positive Sciences Series 1.) It contains Sanskrit text and English translation.

ManuSm Manusmr̥ti = Mānava Dharma-śāstra. The code of Manu. Critically edited by J. Jolly. London 1887.

Masica 1979 C. P. Masica: Aryan and non-Aryan elements in North Indian agriculture. in: Aryan and non-Aryan in India. edited by M. M. Deshpande and P. E. Hook. Ann Arbor 1979, 55–151.

MatsyaP Matsyapurāṇa Bombay 1895 Veṅkateśvara Press; English translation by a Taluqdar of Oudh, Allahabad 1916–1917.

Menon 1903 C. Karunakara Menon: Some agricultural ceremonies in Malabar. in: BMM VI (1903), 98–105.

Meyer 1937 J. J. Meyer: Trilogie altindischer Mächte und Feste der Vegetation. Zürich–Leipzig 1937.

Mishra 1973 N. Mishra: An alphabetical catalogue of Sanskrit manuscripts in the collection of the Orissa State Museum Bhubaneshvar. Bhubaneshvar 1973.

R. Mitra 1871 Rajendralala Mitra: Notices on Sanskrit MSS. Published under orders of the Government of Bengal. Vol. I. Calcutta 1871.

MW M. Monier–Williams: A Sanskrit–English dictionary. Oxford 1960.

NCC New catalogus catalogorum. Edited by V. Raghavan and others. Madras 1949–

Nene Personal communication by Prof. Y. L. Nene, Secunderabad, India.

Nene 2002 Y. L. Nene: Modern agronomic concepts and practices evident in Kautilya's Arthasastra. in: AAH 6:3 (2002), 231–242.

Nene 2004 Y. L. Nene: Commentary. in: Viśvavallabha edited and translated by Nalini Sadhale... 106–114.

NIA New Indian Antiquary

Nilakanta Sastri 1955² K. A. Nilakanta Sastri: The Colas. Madras 1955².

NīlamaP Nīlamatapurāṇa. Ed. by Ved Kumari. Srinagar 1973.

NītiKaT Nītikalpataru ascribed to Vyāsadāsa Kṣemendra. Critically edited by V. P. Mahajan. Poona 1956.

Novikova 1965 V. A. Novikova: Otserky istorii Bengalskoy literatury. Leningrad 1965.

NyāyaMañ Nyāyamañjarī of Jayantabhaṭṭa quoted after Das 1988.

OLZ Orientalische Literaturzeitung

Oppert 1880 Lists of Sanskrit manuscripts in private libraries in southern India. Compiled by G. Oppert. Vol. I. Madras 1880.

Oppert 1885 Lists of Sanskrit manuscripts in private libraries in southern India. Compiled by G. Oppert. Madras 1885.

Padmanabha Menon 1982 K. P. Padmanabha Menon: History of Kerala. Edited by T. K. Krishna Menon. Vol. I. Reprint edition. New Delhi 1982 (first edition: 1924).

PāraGS Pāraskaragṛhyasūtra. Edited by M. G. Bakre. Bombay 1917.

Pingree 1981 D. Pingree: Jyotiḥśāstra. Astrological and mathematical literature. Wiesbaden 1981. (A history of Indian literature VI. 4.)

Pollock 1985 Sh. Pollock: The theory and practice and the practice of theory in Indian intellectual history. in: JAOS 105/3 (1985), 499–519.

pw O. Böhtlingk: Sanskrit Wörterbuch in kürzerer Fassung. St. Petersburg 1879–1889.

Rahman 1982 A. Rahman: Science and technology in medieval India. A bibliography of source materials in Sanskrit, Arabic and Persian. New Delhi 1982.

Rahman 1990 A. Rahman: Science and technology in medieval India. in: History of science and technology in India. Edited by G. Kuppuram K. Kumudamani. Delhi 1990. Volume V, 35–64.

Ramdas 1992 R. V. Ramdas: Glimpses of Kr̥ṣiparraśaraṁ [sic!] (A Sanskrit work devoted exclusively to different agricultural operations). in: Bedekar 1992, 101–106.

RājaT Kalhaṇa's Rājataraṅgiṇī or Chronicle of the kings of Kashmir. Edited by M. A. Stein. Bombay 1892.

Rāmā Rāmāyaṇa . [Edited by] P. R. Śāstri. Kāśi 1959.

Randhawa 1980 M. S. Randhawa: A history of agriculture in India. Vol. I. New Delhi 1980.

Rāya Yogachandra Rāya: Khanā. in: Sāhitya – parishat patrikā. Vol. 10. No. 1. Calcutta 1903.

Ritschl 1980 E. Ritschl: Brahmanische Bauern. Zur Theorie und Praxis der brahmanischen Ständeordnung im alten Indien. in: AOF 7 (1980), 177–187.

Rocher 1986 L. Rocher: The Purāṇas. Wiesbaden 1986. (A history of Indian literature II. 3.)

Roşu 1986 A. Roşu: Mantra et yantra dans la médicine et l' alchimie indiennes. in: JA 274 (1986) 203–268.

Roy 1948 J. C. Roy: Life in ancient India. Calcutta 1948.

RV Die Hymnen des Rigveda. Herausgegeben von T. Aufrecht. Bonn 1877.

Sarkar 1937 B. K. Sarkar: The positive background of Hindu sociology. Allahabad 1937. (first edition 1914)

Sarma 1984 Thakkura Pherū's Rayaṇaparikkhā a medieval Prakrit text on gemmology. Translated with an introduction Sanskrit chāyā and commentary by S. R. Sarma. Aligarh 1984.

Sarma 2001 S. R. Sarma's review on: Sadhale–Balkundi–Nene 1999. in: Traditional South Asian Medicine 6 (2001), 171–173.

K. V. Sarma 1972 K. V. Sarma: A history of the Kerala school of Hindu astronomy. Hoshiarpur 1972.

Schmithausen 1997 L. Schmithausen: Maitrī and magic: aspects of the Buddhist attitude toward the dangerous in nature. Wien 1997.

Sen 1949 D. Sen: Vaṅgabhāṣā sāhitya. 8th edition. Kālikātā 1949.

Sen 1979[3] Sukumar Sen: History of Bengali literature. New Delhi 1979[3].

Sen Gupta 1955 P. C. Sen Gupta: A short note on Khanā's time. in: JRAS(L) XXI. (1955), 59–61.

Sinha 2003 D. P. Sinha: The state in early Indian economy. A study of the Kauṭilya's Arthaśāstra. Patna–New Delhi 2003, 19–65.

Sircar 1965 D. C. Sircar: The sayings of Ḍāk. in: Prāgjyotiṣa Souvenir. Edited by M. Neog. Gauhati 1965, 24–28.

Sivanārayya 1980 N. Sivanārayya: Telugu sahitya kosamu. Haidarābādu 1980.

ŚivataRaK Śivatattva Ratnākara of Basavarāja. Vols. I.–II. Edited by S. Narayanaswamy Sastry. Mysore 1964–1969.

Suguna sri 2004 Personal communication by M. Suguna sri

ŚṛṅgāPra Śṛṅgāraprakāśa of Bhoja ed. by V. Raghavan. Madras 1963.

Stein 1994 B. stein: Peasant state and society in medieval South India. Delhi–Oxford–New York 1994. Oxford India paperback. (first edition: Oxford 1980)

Tivari 1946 S. P. Tivari: Khetī kī kahāvateṅ.1946.

Tripathi 1971 Dh. Tripathi: Prāchyabhāratīyaṁ rituvijñānam. (Ancient Indian science of climatology and weather-forecasting) Varanasi 1971.

R. N. Tripathi 1949 R. N. Tripathi: Ghāgh aur Bhaḍḍarī. [Prayāg] 1949^2.

Tirupati index An alphabetical index of Sanskrit, Telugu and Tamil manuscripts (palm-leaf and paper) in the Sri Venkateswara Oriental Research Institute Library Tirupati. Tirupati 1956.

VaikhāSmS Vaikhānasasmārtasūtram. Critically edited by W. Caland. Calcutta 1927.

Vacek Personal communication by Prof. Jaroslav Vacek (Prague)

Vandhyopadhyay 1893 R. Vandhyopadhyay: A collection of agricultural sayings in lower Bengal with analogous sayings in Bihar and Orissa. Calcutta 1893.

VIJ Vishveshwaranand Institute Journal

Vijayalakshsmi 1993 K. Vijayalakhsmi: Traditional Indian agriculture. An annotated bibliography. New Delhi–Bangalore–Bombay–Calcutta 1993.

VUOJ Sri Venkateswara University Oriental Journal, Tirupati

Wilson 1828^2 H. H. Wilson: The Mackenzie collection. A descriptive catalogue of the Oriental manuscripts... collected by Lieut. Col. Colin Mackenzie. Calcutta 1828.

Winternitz 1967 M. Winternitz: History of Indian literature. II/2 (Scientific literature) transl. from the German into English with additions by Subhadra Jhā. Delhi–Varanasi–Patna 1967.

Wojtilla 1976 Gy. Wojtilla: Kṛṣiparāśara. in: WZHU Gesellschafts- und sprachwissenschaftliche Reihe 35: 3 (1976), 377–378.

Wojtilla–Wojtilla 1976a J. (=Gy) Wojtilla–A. Wojtilla: Reed-symbolism in ancient Egypt and India. in: Studia Aegyptiaca II (Budapest 1976), 145–155. (Études publiées par les Chaires d'Histoire Ancienne de l'Université Loránd Eötvös de Budapest 17.)

Wojtilla 1977 Gy. Wojtilla: The plough as described in the Kṛṣiparāśara. in: AOF (1977), 245–252.

Wojtilla 1977a Gy. Wojtilla: Terminological studies of selected plant names of the Krsiparasara. in: VUOJ XX, January–December 1977, 111–119.

Wojtilla 1982 Gy. Wojtilla: Notes on kṛṣiśāstra. in: VIJ XX: 1–2. (1982), 164–172.

Wojtilla 1982a Gy. Wojtilla: Indian village community according to the Kṛṣiparāśara and some other contemporary sources. in: Les communautés rurales. Rural communities – III: 3 Asie et Islam. Asia and Islam. Paris 1982. (Recueils de la Société Jean Bodin. XLII), 119–129.

Wojtilla 1985 Gy. Wojtilla: Skt. kheṭa- . in: IIJ 28:3, July 1985, 200.

Wojtilla 1986 Gy. Wojtilla: Some problems of the Sankrit terminology of agriculture. in: Sanskrit and World Culture. Proceedings of the Fourth World Sanskrit Conference, Weimar, May 23–30, 1979. Edited by W. Morgenroth. Berlin 1986.

Wojtilla 1988 Gy. Wojtilla: The Sanskrit terminology of the plough. in: AOH 42:2-3. (1988), 325–338.

Wojtilla 1989 Gy. Wojtilla: The ard-plough in ancient and early medieval India. Remarks on its history based on linguistic and archaeological evidence. in: Tools and Tillage 6:2 (1989), 94–106.

Wojtilla 1991 Gy. Wojtilla: The Kṛṣiśāsana. The manual of agricultural implements in Sanskrit. A description of the plough-types. in: Tools and Tillage VII: 4 (Copenhagen 1991), 202–209.

Wojtilla 1991a Gy. Wojtilla: Rural expansion in early medieval India. A linguistic assessment. in: AOF 18 (Berlin 1991), 163–169.

Wojtilla 1993 Gy. Wojtilla: Notes on Daśarathaśāstrin's Kṛṣiśāsana. in: ABORI LXXII–LXXIII (1993), 527–532.

Wojtilla 1995 Gy. Wojtilla: Some remarks on the Kāśyapīyakṛṣisūkti. in: International conference on Sanskrit and related studies September 23–26, 1993 (Proceedings). Cracow 1995, 269–274. (Cracow Indological Studies Vol. I.)

Wojtilla 1997–1998 Gy. Wojtilla: Some remarks on the Sītādhyakṣaprakaraṇa of the Arthaśāstra. in: Indologica Taurinensia XXIII–XXIV (1997–1998), 673–681.

Wojtilla 2001 Gy. Wojtilla's review on Sadhale–Balkundi–Nene 1999. in: Asian Medicine July 2001, 14–16.

Wojtilla 2001a Gy. Wojtilla: New light on the verse 112 of the Kṛṣiparāśara. in: AOH 54: 2–3 (2001), 187–189.

Wojtilla 2002 Gy. Wojtilla: Sanskrit names of plants in the Kāśyapīyakṛṣisūkti. in: AOH 55:4 (2002), 327–333.

Wojtilla 2004 Gy. Wojtilla: Notes on Pākaśāstra, Sūpaśāstra and Sūpaśāstra. In: Studia Asiatica IV (2003)–V (2004), 337–346.

Wojtilla forthcoming Gy. Wojtilla: The Sītādhyakṣaprakaraṇa of the Arthaśāstra.

Wojtilla forthcoming Gy. Wojtilla: A preliminary report on the Kṛṣisamayanirṇaya.

WZHU Wissenschaftliche Zeitschrift der Humboldt-Universität zu Berlin

Zbavitel 1976 D. Zbavitel: Bengali literature. Wiesbaden 1976. (A history of Indian literature IX. 3.)

ZDMG Zeitschrift der Deutschen Morgenländischen Gesellschaft

Zvelebil 1975 K. V. Zvelebil: Tamil literature. Leiden–New York–Köln–Kobenhavn

1975. (Handbuch der Orientalistik II. 2. 1.)

Zvelebil 1995 K. V. Zvelebil: Lexicon of Tamil literature. Leiden–New York–Köln–København 1995. (Handbuch der Orientalistik II. 9.)